THE ART AND CRAFT
OF
Hand Weaving

THE ART AND CRAFT OF Hand Weaving

INCLUDING
Fabric Design

By LILI BLUMENAU

Instructor in Weaving, Teachers College, Columbia University,
and Fashion Institute of Technology

DRAWINGS BY MARTIN NORMAN

CROWN PUBLISHERS, INC. · NEW YORK

Seventh Printing, March, 1971

© COPYRIGHT, 1955, BY LILI BLUMENAU
LIBRARY OF CONGRESS CATALOG CARD NUMBER: 55-7241

PRINTED IN THE UNITED STATES OF AMERICA

ACKNOWLEDGMENTS

I wish to acknowledge and thank the following people and institutions for their kind and valuable assistance in the preparation of this book: Mr. David Sortor, Mrs. Sarah George, Mrs. Camilla Arnold, Miss Suzanne Butzow, Mr. E. S. Rinaldy, Handweaver & Craftsman, United Fruit Company, Cooper Union Museum, New York; The Wool Bureau, New York; National Cotton Council of America, New York; American Viscose Corporation; Jack Lenor Larsen, Inc., New York; Anni Albers.

TABLE OF CONTENTS

INTRODUCTION	1
PART I: EVOLUTION, LOOMS, WEAVING PROCEDURE	
Evolution	3
Loom Parts and their Function	25
Names of Loom Parts	29
Kinds of Looms and Tools	30
Weaving Procedure	38
Glossary of Weaving Preparation	44
PART II: FIBERS	45
General Characteristics	45
Natural Fibers	45
Wool	45
Other Hair Fibers	51
Silk	52
Cotton	54
Linen and Other Bast Fibers	59
Structural Fibers	62
Asbestos	62
Synthetic Fibers	62
Rayon	63
Nylon	66
Resin, Plastic and Glass	66
Yarns	67
Plain Yarns	67
Yarn Count	67
Novelties	68
Dyeing	70
PART III: WEAVES	71
Drafting Symbols of Weaves	72
Drafting	73
Entering or Threading Draws	76

Foundation Weaves	78
Plain Weave	78
Twill Weaves	79
Satin Weave	80
Derivative Weaves	82
Basket Weave	83
Rib Weave	84
Twill Variation	85
Combination Weaves	90
Color Values in Relation to Weave	93
Honeycomb	97
Lace, or Mock Leno	97
Corded Weaves	99
Back Filling and Double Cloth	101
PART IV: DESIGN	103
Yarn	104
Weave Construction	109
Color	112
Weight, or Volume	117
Motif	118
Planning	125
BUYER'S GUIDE	128
BIBLIOGRAPHY	131
INDEX	133

Introduction

THIS BOOK stems from the interest of my students and of many people with whom I have come in contact in weaving. From practical experience in painting, designing and research at Cooper Union Museum, I have written about weaving with the intention of making it interesting and purposeful to many minds.

My ambition is not to add a technical book on weaving. Here are no recipes for making specific cloth, with instructions from beginning to end. There are many books which give such information in detail, ready to copy. Step-by-step information would defeat my purpose which is to suggest the experience gained in practicing this craft, the joy that comes from study and self-discovery.

Craftsmen have rediscovered the frustration of developing a skill that leads only to machine-like precision. Technique, in this case the knowledge of weaving mechanics, can be taken for granted as the foundation for creative work. But it is not the only means to an end, for the real emphasis in weaving is on the visual and tactile characteristics of raw material—yarn, weave, color. Twentieth century handweaving is vital and independent. But creative invention has always been based on an awareness of the character of the individual elements of yarns —their stiffness or softness, diagonal or zigzag in weaves, the brightness or dullness of colors.

I have tried to show how a weaver-designer invents surface in textiles through variation, small with large squares, dark with light, and so on, depending on ability, effort and trained seeing. This kind of creation is open to everyone. It is not restricted to special artists.

Included among my intended readers, however, are those who professionally work with and deal with textiles. This book, which is meant for all kinds of people, may inspire a housewife or a businessman to begin weaving. I have sought to satisfy normal curiosity about how textiles are made. Home weavers, stylists and students should be able to find new ideas and a new outlook. Teachers may find my point of view useful as a basis in education, especially in showing history as a record of man's creative capacity through weaving.

There is extraordinary interest in handweaving today, when mechanization, speed and specialization seem to dominate the field, perhaps because the mechanical world has begun to make many people feel like robots, and these people experience a need to do things inspired by themselves, not planned and dictated for them by collective standards.

Handweaving appeals both to the practical and artistic in people. But there is a tendency to practice it as a hobby, which puts it on a negative level. Begun as a leisure activity, however, weaving may become a practical and profitable endeavor. And, as a result of the study of textiles as a practicing handweaver, industrial careers have and can be made. Thinking, based on knowledge, about design and quality develops both talent and feeling in this craft. Then, of course, textiles improve our surroundings, make us see other beauty in life.

My writing is especially an invitation to men and women who are looking for a leisure activity in which they are both planner and producer. As briefly as possible I have arranged the technical essentials and ideas of weaving as an expression of idea in yarn and color. The creative imagination and color instincts in everyone are always brought out in weaving and may be guided to worthwhile, sometimes inspired, expression.

The ideal of handweaving today is not simply material. It is a means of self-realization and fulfillment. And its purpose today is unique. Practically, we do not need to weave cloth by hand but the value of weaving is in the work. The present-day desire to weave is one expression of the search in our time for human qualities.

Part I. Evolution, Looms, Weaving

THE STORY of textiles, old and complex, is a testament to man's evolution. Weaving is a record of our aptitudes, of our individual talents, of our progress, which began in remote times and to meet a basic need for clothing. Out of the natural struggle to take care of necessities grew the civilizing desire for improvement and perfection of self.

Interlacing of fibers, which is weaving, may have begun even before the age of agriculture, ten or twelve thousand years ago, during the Neolithic age of which we are a part. In telling the story, one can select only the highlights of known developments and the important areas of invention in textile history. But weaving is not limited to tools, looms, materials and power machines. It includes ornament and design, which are of historical and artistic importance.

Art historians, whose work is to arrange facts and events chronologically while suggesting cause and effect, are our authority. Their source is the archaeologist who collects, classifies, and compares tools and productions of various ages. From these materials prehistory is scientifically formulated and made part of our heritage.

The archaeological time-span during which the first textiles were created is enormous, not measurable in years and centuries but in units of thousands and tens of thousands of years.

The museum fragments of textiles, woven about 1800 years ago in Egypt or Peru, cause us to speculate. Perhaps we are astonished that so long ago people had discovered threadmaking from raw material and had made looms to convert that thread into cloth. For us, these fragments of cloth have a life and spirit beyond the practical necessity for which they were created. They are the product of weavers of great artistic invention and they tell us as well something of peoples' lives and taste in various eras.

Differing opinions will always exist concerning the origin and first examples of weaving. Perhaps weaving began in many places simultaneously, but the actual place-source is unknown and even archaeologists cannot fully enlighten us.

Weaving began a long time before the oldest known paintings of weavers and looms in Egypt—about 2000 B.C. Prehistoric household implements excavated in Switzerland during the last century suggest that the first real weaving could not have been during the earliest stages of human development. Textile making was impossible while man was still a hunter and constantly moving to escape danger. Weaving required repose and probably developed only after men, such as the Swiss lake dwellers, had begun to establish settlements.

The answer to man's need to invent and improve his inventions lies in the necessities created by his circumstances. He cultivated plants, tamed animals, cooked his food, built houses and heated them. But just as important was the security necessary for learning self-control and exercising his imagination. Invention or improvement also take place when a desire for something better, including relief from discomfort, inspires a new use for materials and objects. In any case, the desire to improve is more than a wish for money or fame.

The pre-weaving era saw the development

of skills in matting and basketry—Paleolithic work of twenty to forty thousand years ago. The Neolithic, New Stone Age, which followed, is the present age which saw the invention of the loom and spinning devices. Much later in this period, and for the first time in human history, we developed our skill for technical invention and worldwide trade for profit. This development was the first industrial revolution, known as the Renaissance, and was followed by a more widespread industrial revolution which saw the use of the power-speed weaving systems and machinery which now dominate modern weaving.

In the pre-weaving era, which we can only imagine, man was a hunter and killed to live. As he began to control his environment, his need and his ability to invent increased. He began to make original uses of nature's raw materials.

Weaving may have begun with building shelters. The houses of the post-hunting period were windbreaks, constructed by driving upright branches into the ground, side by side, joined and fortified with horizontal branches at regular intervals. Then the builders wove grasses over and around the uprights (*Fig. 1*).

Perhaps from the solid planes of this primitive housing grew the idea of making and hanging mats as additional insulation against the wind and protection against cold earth floors. These early ancestors were also wanderers, who needed carriers for their children, food and other household portables, and they found that by bending and joining plaited and twined mats, they could make such carriers which were, in effect, baskets.

Fig. 1. Grasses tied with strips of palm leaf. Egyptian, Late Dynastic Period. *Metropolitan Museum of Art.*

Fig. 2. Basket of split palm leaves, grasses, and string. Egyptian, Empire Period. *Metropolitan Museum of Art.*

In primitive plaiting, twining and basketry, two distinct sets of long units were combined by the process of interlacing more or less at right angles (*Fig. 3*). The process of crossing a horizontal over a vertical material was done stitch by stitch. The materials were

EVOLUTION

manipulated over and under, or around, each vertical branch or stick. Later, in weaving, it was the same kind of interlacing but accomplished more efficiently by the simple alternating movement of raising even and odd sets of material to admit the weft. For basketry techniques, no tools were needed, only materials such as reeds, grasses and sticks, more or less as they are found in nature. The tool for combining them was the hand.

As our ancestors grew more dependent on the usefulness and comfort provided by rugs and baskets, they began to find ways to make

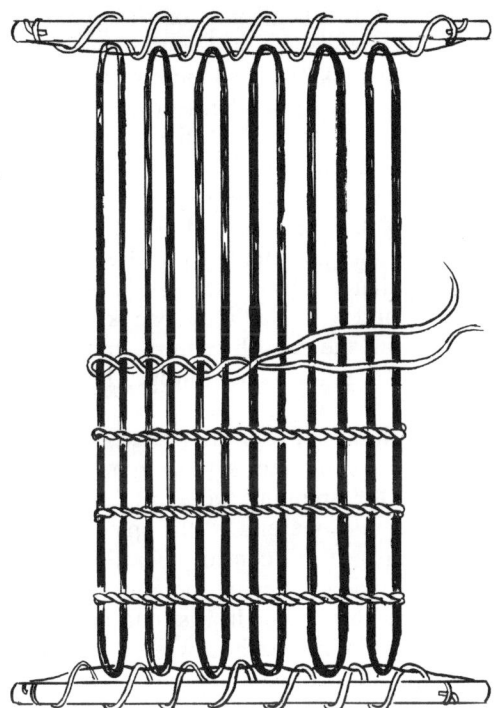

Fig. 3. Twining technique on lengthwise stretched material.

Fig. 4. Contemporary Cherokee basket weaving. *Handweaver and Craftsman* Magazine. *Photo, Cherokee Historical Assn.*

Fig. 5. Twined basket in process. Pomo Indians, California. *Smithsonian Institution.*

softer, more pliable fabrics of a larger size, fabrics which were eventually used as clothing and for personal adornment to replace leaves and skins. Soft materials called for short, hairlike fibers of a kind found in reeds and other plants. The next discovery was to join these fibers in lengths of usable thread. The only finished thread provided by nature, the thread spun by the silkworm, was not yet discovered. And the early people had to invent spinning—the step at which weaving history begins.

The curly wool of sheep, the first domesticated animals, was perhaps the source of the earliest short, hairlike units to be developed into long yarns. While sheep bones are found at the Neolithic levels of Swiss Lake culture, there is no evidence that spun sheep's wool was used for textiles. The first use of wool in cloth in Europe was about 2500 B.C. Early domestication of sheep is well known from the Bible and Sumerian wall mosaics of 3500 B.C.

Whether of wool, linen or cotton, we can be sure that the first twisting or spinning of short units was simple. The bunches of tangled fibers were straightened by hand. Then, while holding one of these masses in his left hand, the spinner twisted and lengthened the material into a fairly even yarn which had the disadvantage of falling apart. The spinner finally prevented this by winding the finished thread around a stick, notched to secure it as he wound and twisted. When this tool, ultimately the spindle, slipped from his hand the thread unwound. This awkwardness, in turn, gave him the idea of making the thread wind itself, so he rotated the spindle instead of winding the thread around it.

In order to maintain spindle rotation, a weight, or whorl, was attached to the lower end of the spindle. The whorl served as flywheel (originally a stone ring) and prevented the thread from slipping off the spindle. At the beginning of the spinner's operation, the straightened, carded wool was placed on a stick and held loosely in position by means of a thread. This device was the origin of the distaff, which the spinner later carried under his left arm, or in his belt, so he could move about while spinning.

Spinning with spindle and distaff is represented in antique painting on Greek vases and Egyptian tombs (*Figs.* 6, 7). The ancient method was the only one known in Europe until the twelfth century, and is still practiced by peasants in Europe, Peru and Mexico (*Fig.* 8).

The earliest spinners discovered that cotton required a different system from the system used for spinning wool or flax. They learned to rest one end of the spindle on a smooth surface to control vibration. The fibers, twisted together by the fingers of one hand, were drawn out in a strong and continuous yarn. This method was practiced in the early days of the cotton industry in India, and the Hindus were able to make all the fine yarns for sheer muslin. Indian cotton spinning spread to West Africa and the Philippines and was also used in Peru, before the Incas, where it is still used as it was originally.

The extraordinary fact about the history of looms is that their basic structure has not altered in five thousand years. There has been no need. Looms were devised by our ancestors simply to control the long new spun yarns in manageable position. After the introduction of the spindle and distaff, the short or limited units of grasses and reeds were displaced by spun threads. The task, then, was to unite these long yarns in such a way as to produce a large plane of fabric. Combining horizontals with verticals had already been discovered in plaiting and basketry but only for stiff materials. The new pliable yarn lengths required stretched position or tension to be interlaced.

Fig. 6. Weaving and spinning. Egyptian wall painting, XII Dynasty. *Metropolitan Museum of Art.*

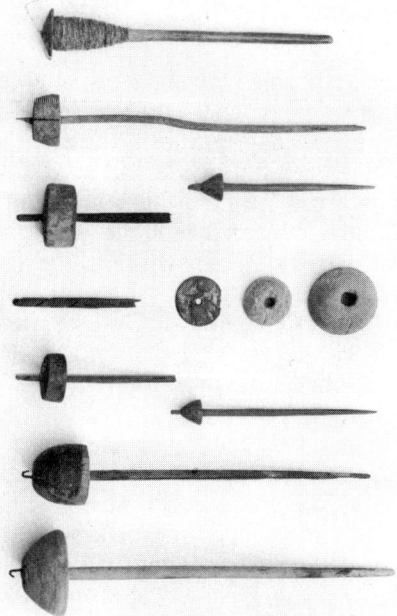

Fig. 7. Egyptian spinning implements. *Metropolitan Museum of Art.*

Fig. 8. Italian peasant spinning with distaff and spindle. *Smithsonian Institution.*

The first looms were not complex: a pair of sturdy upright beams secured to the floor and united at the top with a crossbeam. A warping system was made by using a very long thread, loosely guided from top to bottom over the crossbeam. The thread was continuous and long enough to form the width of the material. In order to hold this lengthwise yarn taut, small bunches were weighted with stones or other heavy objects. This loom appears on Greek vases made in 600 B.C. and is the kind usually associated with Penelope (*Fig. 9*).

In order to weave the warp with crosswise yarns, some of the weighted threads were lifted so that the weft could be passed in one movement through the divided warp. Perhaps, at first, a flat stick was used to raise the alternating lengthwise threads. By slanting the stick, the weft was inserted from right to left—a slow process that soon developed into a more progressive idea: the heddle rod.

The earliest models of this long rod were possibly the same length as the width of the loom. The rod was placed across and on top of the warp yarns. A long string was fastened around the beginning of the heddle rod and guided under a warp around the rod and continued under the alternating warp end. When the rod system was perfected, a permanent warp-lifting device had been created. One had only to lift the stick to raise the odd-numbered yarns in one movement. Another stick was used to lift the even-numbered threads for the following weft. After the wefts were made they were pressed together with a piece of wood, or other tool. Weaving on the warp-weighted loom was done upwards, the wefts pressed away from the weaver, not toward him, as in present usage.

The looms and weaving tools of Greece and Egypt were practically the same as those used by Pre-Incan Peruvian weavers. In fact, these looms are still in use and consist simply of two rods to hold the warp in place. The length and breadth of the warp yarns between the two rods comprises the loom. One end is hitched to a post and the other to the belt of the weaver. As the weaver moves back, the warp tightens and he begins weaving, seated on the ground (*Figs.* 10, 11).

With such unbelievably simple looms and spindles were produced the beautiful fabrics we see and admire today in museums. Most of the few remaining Egyptian fabrics are mummy wrappings of fine natural linen thread. The late Egyptian or Coptic Christian weavers (300 to 700 A.D.) produced colorful figure-decorated textiles in tapestry

Fig. 9. Upright loom with weighted warp. Athenian vase, about 500 B.C. *Metropolitan Museum of Art.*

EVOLUTION

Fig. 10. Girdle loom with heddle rod and stick, with alternate warp yarns lifted in succession.

Fig. 11. Guatemalan girdle looms. Compare with drawing. *United Fruit Company.*

of the simple, mending type of weave. We can see in these fragments parts of the tunics customarily worn during this period, decorated with scenes from Greek mythology, geometrical motifs, and Christian scenes or Christian emblems, such as the monogram of Christ and the Alpha and Omega (*Figs.* 12, 13).

European weaving was based on the Egyptian cultures combined with the influence of Persian design of the Sassanid dynasty (600 to 700 A.D.). The Persian weavers are believed to have learned their intricate patterns from the Chinese. Still later influences were Byzantine, which itself was influenced by Saracenic, or Arabic, weaving.

The influence of Oriental textiles on European design was constant. Sassanid and Byzantine design, which is formal, but manages to represent or suggest objects, was especially popular. The underlying plan in Oriental textiles consisted of circular bands or roundels, repeated at more or less regular intervals.

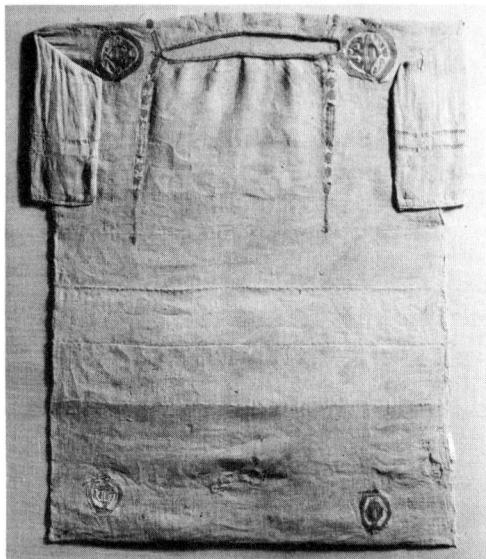

Fig. 12. Coptic child's tunic. Natural linen, plain weave, decorated with tapestry-woven motifs in bright color. Egyptian, 5th century. *Cooper Union Museum.*

Fig. 13. Tapestry-woven Coptic motif in dark purple wool on linen tunic. Egyptian, 5th century. *Cooper Union Museum.*

The spaces within and around the circles are decorated with animals (*Fig.* 14), fantastic and real, some facing each other, or placed back to back. In the thirteenth or fourteenth centuries, the circular framework was elongated, approaching ogival form, characteristic of the Gothic.

Arabic, Italian and Spanish weavers made their designs either with or without roundels, reflecting Persian and Byzantine custom. The framework often contained Arabic inscriptions, rosettes and geometric forms. The absence of animal forms in many of the Arabic textiles is because of religious interdiction by the Sunni Mohammedans. A second more fruitful dogma forbidding the use of large quantities of silk, introduced by way of China and Persia, resulted in the unique weaving of stripes of linen with silk, often decorated, and of silk motifs on linen background.

Also, about this time, the hitherto simple interlacing techniques, or stitches, became

Fig. 14. Byzantine silk twill, Persian influence, 11th century. *Cooper Union Museum.*

elaborate. From plain weave, mending style, grew weft twill, diagonal, as well as double cloth, which was very popular. Weft-revealing weaves were evolved from tapestry technique, in order to conceal the warp, as is necessary in figure weaving (*Figs.* 15, 16, 17).

This period in advanced weaving was by far the greatest in textile history. It includes the cultivation of natural fibers, basic spinning and weaving techniques, the invention of new weaves, the introduction of motifs and investigation and greater use of natural dyes. It was the first industrial revolution, and it began about the end of the fourteenth century when, for the first time, technical invention and worldwide trade for profit promoted each other. Out of India came the spinning wheel and foot-treadle loom; out of China, the long-hidden secret of silk-reeling, as well as the earliest type of draw loom for

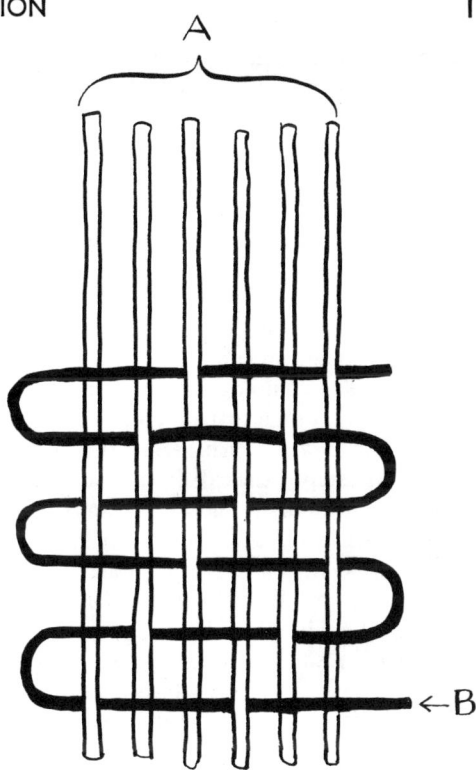

Fig. 16. Diagram of weft twill. A, warp. B, weft.

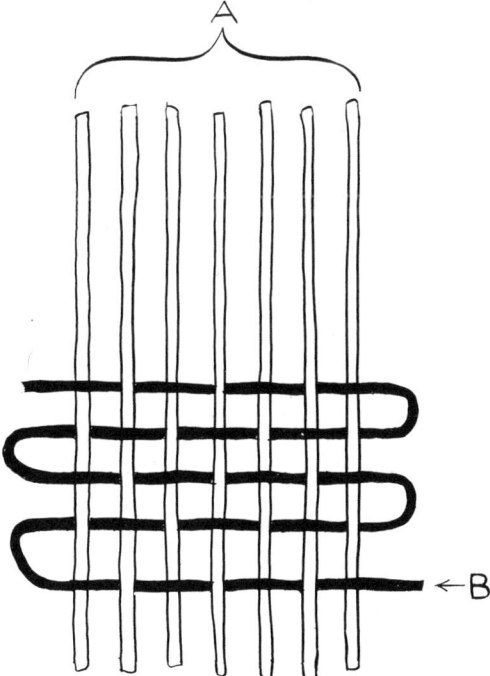

Fig. 15. Diagram of plain weave. A, warp. B, weft.

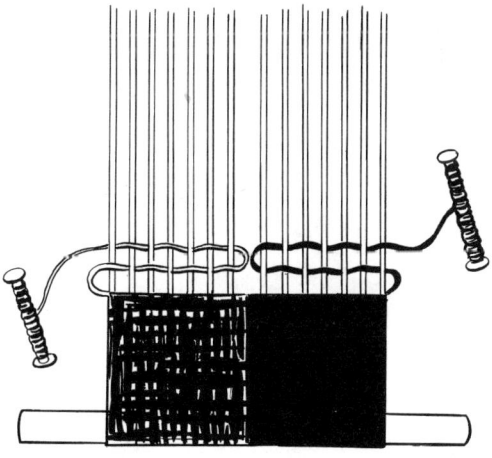

Fig. 17. Tapestry weaving. In this technique, weft yarns of different colors cover parts of warp threads to form design, instead of passing across entire warp as in ordinary weaving.

weaving intricate figures. The French took the draw loom and made fundamental changes to reduce the amount of labor necessary to produce patterned textiles. (The French chemists, in the early eighteenth century, also began extensive experiment in dyestuff.)

The new adjuncts to weaving were crude and unproductive, compared with their nineteenth and twentieth century offspring, yet they represented an immense advance in technology. The spinning wheel of India, for example, was a crude instrument, capable of making only coarse yarns. But this wheel was a long step forward from the distaff method which had supplied yarn until then.

The whorl, after the fourteenth century, was converted into a big wheel, the spindle attached to it by a belt which caused it to revolve as the wheel revolved. Later, a large wheel drove a smaller one that turned the spindle by means of a wharve, a small, grooved pulley, fastened to the end of the spindle (*Figs.* 18, 19).

The wheel-spinning method consisted of

Fig. 19. Flax-spinning wheel. United States, early 19th century. *The New York Historical Society.*

Fig. 18. Wool-spinning wheel. United States, early 19th century. *The New York Historical Society.*

three motions: drawing (attenuating) the fibers, twisting, and, finally, winding them on a spindle. The preliminary was fiber-carding with combs to change the fiber mass of cotton or wool into soft rolls a foot or more

Fig. 20. Pair of wool cards, or combs. United States, early 19th century. *The New York Historical Society.*

in length. The spinner, standing at the wheel, drew and twisted a short length from the roll, or film, and fastened it to the spindle. Next, he wound the twisted end around the point of the spindle and held the rest of the roll in his left hand. The wheel was then turned with a stick, later the handle, and the spindle brought into motion. The spinner gently drew the filmy roll away from the spindle almost in line with it. As the roll became attenuated, the spindle twisted it into yarn, in the same way that the revolving vertical spindle had twisted it by the whorl and distaff hand method.

After a bunch of fibers had been drawn and twisted almost to its end, the worker stopped the wheel and revolved it slowly in the opposite direction. The spun yarn, extending to the end of the spindle, backed off the center of the spindle or off any point the spinner desired. Again turning his wheel in the original direction, the worker wound the length of spun yarn on the spindle. Now he was ready for another piece of bunched fiber. He laid one end of it over the end of the one just spun, again drawing the end of the twisted part of the yarn to the end of the spindle, and continued.

The spinning wheel was a great advance. It did not strain the yarn by winding it while it was being drawn and twisted. This simple, medieval wheel was the progenitor of the modern spinning mule, the motion of which is also intermittent. On the great wheel one could make several times as much yarn in a given time as with distaff and spindle. Such production relieved the growing demand for yarn, but at the same time there was a new challenge for improvement. Another device was needed to make stronger warp yarns, and its first appearance may have been in Germany, about 1530. This innovation, called the Saxony wheel, was elaborate. A foot treadle was used for revolving the wheel. The hands, consequently, were free to draw fibers and guide them to the spindle. The Saxony wheel was readily used in flax spinning, since the principles of drawing, twisting and winding were continuous. The consequent strain of this wheel on the yarn was negligible, as flax can support tension better than wool or cotton.

Looms, too, were improved, undergoing many changes in the fifteenth and sixteenth centuries. At first, they were simple frames with the warp strung upright, manipulated by heddle rods. A new idea from China made the warp horizontal, with a warp-lifting device more automatic than its predecessors. The frame of the Chinese loom was like a house without walls or roof—four uprights reinforced at top and sides by horizontal beams or braces. The warp was stretched between two rollers fastened at either end of the loom, not far above the floor.

In this loom the heddles, or warp-lifting devices, were longer and tied over two long flat sticks. The warp yarns were threaded through eyes in the center of the heddles. Half the warp was drawn through eyes in one frame, or shaft, and the alternate, or even-numbered, ends through the next frame, back of the first.

The frames in the Chinese loom hung loosely from a crossbeam. At the bottom of each flat stick, or shaft, a string was tied and joined to a pedal. When the weaver pushed one pedal, half the warp threads were lowered and ready for weft insertion. When the other pedal was pushed, the alternate, or even-numbered warp went down, making the plain or mending type of weave (*Fig. 22*).

But on the new loom the wefts had still to be beaten into the cloth by combs or other short tools. The warp rollers were too light to hold such material, yet the yardage had to be long, in comparison with periods when all that was required in weaving was a hanging or a tunic. The small fork for beating the weft was gradually transformed into a long

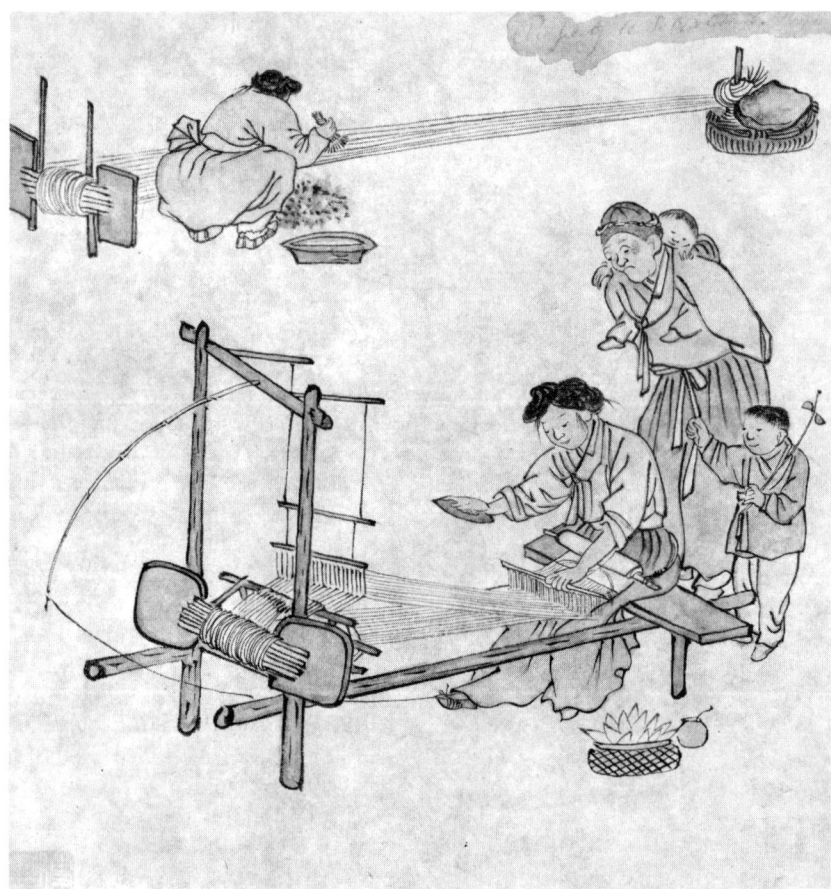

Fig. 21. Chinese primitive weaving. Drawing, 18th century. *Smithsonian Institution.*

Fig. 22. Floor loom with heddle shafts and treadles. Pennsylvania, 1819. *Smithsonian Institution.*

comb set in a frame hung from the top of the loom. Warp yarns, after having been drawn through the heddle eyes, were passed through the comb dents and fastened in front of the loom. The weaver could beat the weft in one even motion—the comb, or reed, being as wide as the loom.

Renaissance weavers were aware of the technical limitation of shaft looms when they tried to weave elaborately figured fabrics. They were looking for a more intricate loom, such as the draw loom already used in Asia about the sixth century.

Figured satins and brocades of the East and West have always been woven on the draw loom principle. Even the Jacquard machine of the early nineteenth century did not alter essentials of draw loom weaving. Before Jacquard, a narrow perforated board was fixed across the loom to replace the heddles. Below the perforations in this board, separate weighted leashes were hung, so arranged that a design occupying the whole width of the loom for one lateral repeat, took no more space than a set of eight or ten shafts in the very smallest patterns. The mechanism of the draw loom may be compared to a puppet theater. The device consists of warp threads lifted by a pulley. It was manipulated by draw boys, at first, and later by a mechanical system.

Products woven on early modern shaft and draw looms differed from fabrics of the early centuries. Indeed, there was a great difference between plain cloth woven for daily use and figured precious silks that were symbols of wealth. However, Renaissance ornamentation began to give way to more realistic styles of design during the seventeenth and eighteenth centuries.

During the Renaissance favorable political and social conditions as well as greater organization of trade and manufacture produced a system of patronage which fostered the arts. Fashion, a modern trend, required extensive production and meant the employment of many more weavers. The fifteenth century, too, witnessed a new weave construction—velvet copied from rugs woven in the Orient, according to inventories of the fourteenth century. Europeans, for the first time, wore a material with a pile. The pile in European velvet, however, was original and was added to the growing number of textiles.

Influence of the Orient on velvet as well as on silk manufacture in Europe cannot be underestimated. Constantinople was for a long time the chief market for supplying silks to the Italian centers. Imported textiles from Byzantium, Persia and Syria stimulated Italian weaving. A leaf shape, with reversed curved lines, became the basic European design of the Renaissance. Within this leaf, and also in ogival form, a fruit ornament, usually a pomegranate, was inserted. Also conspicuous was the first attempt to create all-over simplified woven patterns in the form of wavy lines running vertically, or obliquely, the length of a fabric (*Fig.* 23).

During the sixteenth century, the Oriental tradition was still dominant but there was less formality in the motifs. A demand for greater variety and rapid production account

Fig. 23. Renaissance velvet. Dark green, leaf and pomegranate. Italian, 15th century. *Cooper Union Museum.*

for some of the disappearance of the older, more tranquil weaving schemes, especially in apparel fabrics. Imaginative design died out, and products of unsteady, less-lasting quality began to appear. A greater emphasis on mechanical means of composition at the expense of weaving expression became habitual.

Toward the beginning of the seventeenth century there was a wide use of botanical subjects with here and there a Persian flavor—of little character, however, and entirely different from the early Oriental textiles. The Eastern manner was becoming a habit. A rich mixture of framework, variations of ogival and circular, surrounded the formal and realistic motifs. The great demand for decorated silk and the decline of interest in production of textiles for special customers, account for the decadence which overtook silk weaving in the seventeenth century.

In earlier times, style had been insured by the design of individual textiles. By the sixteenth century, weavers were producing in quantity, with a less clear and immediate sense of the use or purpose of their creations. Mechanized woven designs were made without reference to textile qualities. Seventeenth century effects, baroque in style and architecturally contrived, were especially reflected in a weave called brocatelle. Designs inspired by relief motifs meant for wrought iron and adapted to textiles appeared in other weaves.

The eighteenth century introduced a new surface quality, using shaded motifs, resembling painting, which met with public acclaim. Birds, wheat and wreaths, as designed by Philippe de la Salle, about 1770, were like a painting reproduced in woven silk. Taste was also beguiled by tricks in mixed weaves. There was little sense of form or fitness in this virtuosity and for the first time there was a rift between designer-stylist and weaver. The designers, unacquainted with the limitations of the loom, left problems of construction to technicians.

In addition to these brocade innovations which imitated embroidery and the use of lace designs as motifs, eighteenth century art also introduced scenic and large floral motifs in textiles—crowded patterns manufactured in mass yardage.

Similar floral groups and garlands with serpentine and interlaced ribbons were introduced in the mid-eighteenth century, in light, delicate effects, combined with vertical stripes. This is the fashion associated with French extravagance prior to the revolution. It was followed by plain stripes, combined with bunches, or spots, of small flowers, characteristic ornamentation of the reign of Louis XVI.

Fig. 24. Baroque brocatelle. Italian, 16th century. *Cooper Union Museum.*

Fig. 25. Brocade. White silk decorated with multi-colored, gold and silver flowers. French, 18th century. *Cooper Union Museum.*

All of the silk brocades, brocatelles and damasks were handwoven on the Oriental type of draw loom. The techniques of spinning and weaving were substantially the same as practiced in the middle ages. Limited by the amount of manual labor available, the daily output of spinning wheel and loom could not meet the demand for materials.

Gradually, attempts were made to improve loom and wheel to speed production. The trials to improve the tools of weaving were a considerable part of the fever of mechanical invention later known as the Industrial Revolution.

About 1754, John Kay, of Burry, England, invented the fly shuttle (*Fig. 26*) which

Fig. 26. Model of the first fly shuttle loom, 18th century. Troughlike boxes at left and right of reed form passage, or guide, for shuttle throwing. *Smithsonian Institution.*

first stimulated modern mass production. His mechanization was a pulley system in which shuttle and weft were placed in a box attached to the end of the beater. The weaver, seated at the middle of the loom, pulled a cord connected to the box, and the shuttle was thrown mechanically back and forth through the warp.

The reed was also improved. The teeth of this comb had formerly been made of cane. The new reed consisted of metal dents, durable and well adapted to weaving finer and stronger cloth.

John Kay's invention increased productivity to a degree that unbalanced the relation between the spinning of yarn and the production of cloth and sparked eighteenth century inventors to still more productive inventions in spinning.

A solution for faster spinning came from James Hargreave, a weaver living in England in 1760. He conceived this as a result of a domestic accident. His child overturned a spinning wheel and Hargreave noticed that the spindle revolved long after the wheel had been put back in upright position. He realized that if a number of spindles were placed upright, side by side, controlled by one wheel, many threads might be spun at the same time. He worked on this idea for three years, developing a wheel that was subsequently patented and named for his daughter Jenny (*Fig. 27*).

Threads on the jenny could be made

Fig. 27. Spinning jenny, 1764, showing row of spindles and hand-operated wheel. *The Wool Bureau, New York.*

quicker than ever before, but these yarns were not strong enough for warping. Weavers continued to have to wait for warp to be spun on the slow wheels and were obliged to look for further inventions, so that they could keep up with the fly shuttle weavers.

A young barber, Richard Arkwright, became interested in the spinners' problem. As he listened to them and watched them work, he had an idea that resulted in a spinning machine which made strong thread quickly. Not only did Arkwright invent a better machine than the jenny, but he became the owner of a spinning mill. His machines were too heavy to be worked manually, so he devised means to run them by horse and water power. Arkwright's financial and executive genius was used constructively. He advanced the English textile industry to a point difficult for other nations to overtake. His rise from barber to manufacturer is a story typical of the later industrial age, but unusual in his own.

With all the progress in machinery and working systems, spinning and weaving was still largely a home industry. The children who learned spinning and weaving early were often responsible for improvements and inventions. Samuel Crompton was one of these. As a young man he had been obliged to help his mother spin, although he himself was interested in music, mathematics and books. The fact that he was scolded for losing time joining threads doubtless was the goad that inspired his improvements of the spinning jenny.

Recalling the six years he worked on his idea, Crompton wrote: "My mind was in a continual endeavor to realize a more perfect spinning principle, and, though often baffled, I as often renewed the attempt, and at last succeeded to my utmost desire at the expense of every shilling I had in the world."

His work consisted of combining the good points of the spinning jenny and the horse power frame. Crompton remembered how spinners had at first destroyed the machines Kay and Hargreave made in order to protect themselves against machine competition. To avoid a similar fate for his invention, he sold it to a group of manufacturers who constructed a number of machines based on his idea. They never paid him. The Crompton mule, now in wide use, was a good spinner, but it required skilled workers. Since they knew they could not be replaced by untrained hands, their demand for excessive wages immediately caused manufacturers to look for spinning frames unskilled workers could handle.

Richard Roberts, in 1830, invented such a machine: a self-actor mule that women and children could operate. Another spinner, also easy to handle, was produced about this time by an American. This was the ring spinner, which in mills today is an enormous machine that spins about 1,200 times as much in a day as the early model. The ring spinner draws textile fibers into a loose, untwisted rope (roving) that is pulled and twisted until it has been spun into fine, strong thread.

Faster spinning called for greater quantities of raw material. English ships in American ports brought more and more orders for cotton. In the American South, men talked of the fortunes that could be made raising cotton if there was a faster way of removing the seeds from the fiber. It took a slave a day to clean a pound, so plantation owners urgently sought an answer to their problem.

The solution came toward the end of the eighteenth century after a New England school teacher, Eli Whitney, took a job teaching children on a Georgia plantation. His employer saw that the teacher was inventive and asked him to work on a device for cleaning cotton. While thinking of this, Whitney is said to have observed a cat trying to reach through the bars of a chicken coop and only succeeding in getting its claws full of feathers. From this the inventor is supposed to have learned that the way to separate seeds from cotton was to draw the fiber through an opening too small for the seeds.

The first Whitney model was a drum set with hooks, or barbs, which turned against a grate. Seed cotton was fed into the drum and the hooks caught the fiber, pulling it through a fine screen which left the seeds behind. This invention, the cotton gin, was highly praised by Washington and Jefferson. Whitney tried to patent and manufacture the machine, but could not protect it. The cotton gin was too important at that moment to be kept private. It was copied widely and Whitney waited a long time, through many lawsuits, before he received any reward for his extremely valuable invention.

The spinning machines not only called for more raw material but also for faster looms, a demand that began after 1785, when Edmund Cartwright invented the power loom. Cartwright observed that the handweavers could not keep pace with the supply of material produced by faster spinning. In conversation, he is reputed to have said, "Before long, we shall have weaving johnnies as well as spinning jennies." But the spinners were convinced that a weaving machine would never replace human hands.

Cartwright set to work, and, in spite of knowing little about loom construction, finished a model and took out a patent. He discovered, however, that his loom, compared with hand looms, was difficult to operate. He then worked six years on an automatic machine that was easier to handle and started a factory to manufacture them.

Textile workers did not like Cartwright's "iron men." Weavers saw that this machine could weave more material in a day than they could produce in a week. Many of the first machines were destroyed, but the power loom was accepted by businessmen. More

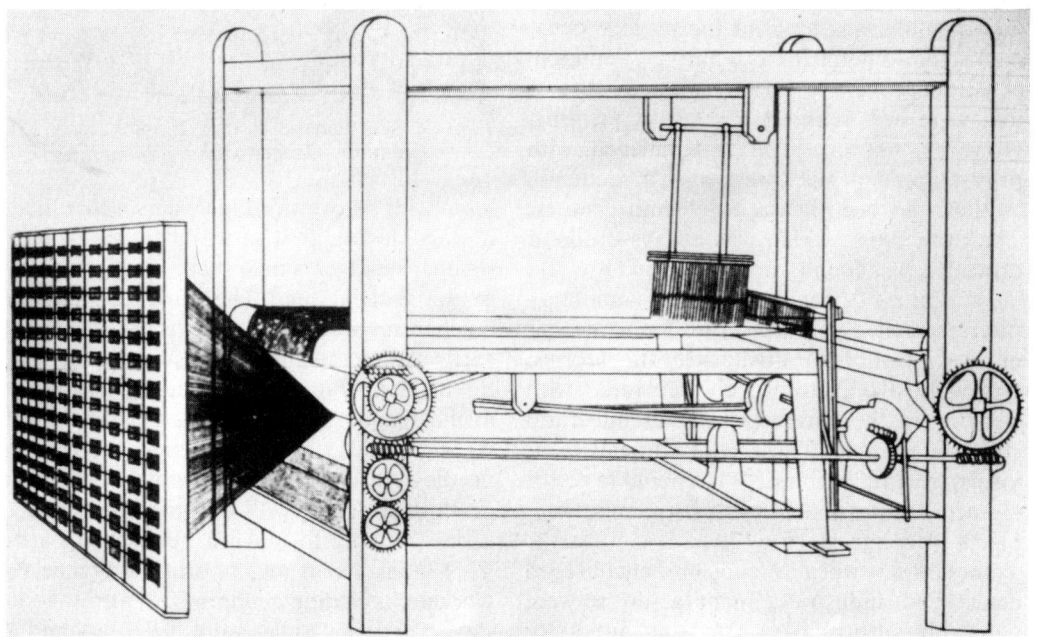

Fig. 28. Cartwright's loom, 1785, with spool rack of warp threads. *The Wool Bureau, N. Y. C.*

and more spinning mills, as well as cloth factories, were built. Cartwright had astonished the spinners and weavers, and answered nineteenth century weaving needs.

Other developments as old as loom and spindle accompanied the rise of weaving machinery. Cast iron and steam power came of age with the new looms and made them possible. The automatic weaving machinery was so powerful in action that only iron parts could stand the strain. Loom parts, such as the beater, were too heavy to be moved except by steam power. It was this astounding coordination of invention which produced the industrial age: iron-working required coal, coal mining required water pumps, and water pumps, steam engines. Such simultaneous development made automatic mechanical weaving possible.

In the early nineteenth century, new spinning and weaving machines produced such an endless stream of textiles, it was necessary to create a greater variety in design. The first solution was to print fabric with ornaments too fanciful for ordinary power loom construction. These yardages, chiefly of cotton, were woven and decorated by printing. However, not everyone was satisfied with prints. Precious silks were also in demand, as they had been in the eighteenth century. The draw loom, which was always used for brocades, was found unproductive in a world of machines. Nineteenth century manufacturers searched for new draw loom mechanisms in order to create elegant fabrics, especially silk, picturesquely decorated with weaving in the Directoire and architectural styles of the day. These new artificial fashions were a reflection of Napoleonic taste for Graeco-Roman and Egyptian ornament, emblems of conquest (*Fig.* 29).

In 1805, when Napoleon encouraged crafts and industries, manufacturers were agreeably surprised by the contribution of Charles Marie Jacquard who invented a draw

Fig. 29. Silk damask. French Empire, early 19th century. *Cooper Union Museum.*

loom with an overhead mechanism that made it possible to lift a few warp threads at a time, instead of small successive groups as in the shaft system. The intricate Jacquard mechanism worked by means of perforated cards pressed against needles connected with the heddles (*Fig.* 30). The card perforations in the Jacquard system represent the design. At each pick, a card presses against the needles, lifting the appropriate warps. To produce a design with this mechanism, it is necessary only to make a new set of cards. This loom meant an important advance for workers, including children, from draw loom slavery where heddles were lifted by hand at the direction of a foreman. Because of Jac-

EVOLUTION

Fig. 30. Modern Jacquard loom. Invented about 1805, to weave intricate designs. Typical punched cards, or warp-lifting pattern, hang above row of heddles. *National Cotton Council of America.*

quard, Lyons became the art center of the textile industry.

After the eighteenth century, there was mechanical equipment for spinning and weaving almost everything needed in textiles. This naturally created changes in the ways people worked. Craftsmen, unable to sell their work, took jobs in factories. More and more mills were built, needing more raw materials and markets.

With every invention the factories were able to turn fibers into cloth more quickly. England, early in this development, could not furnish enough wool—and had no cotton—for rapid production. Britons became sheep ranchers in Australia, New Zealand, Canada and South Africa where they were highly successful at producing the wool needed in England. Furnishing the machines with cotton was a more involved problem. The first of this fiber came from India and the United States. The demand was so great that farmers in the southern United States planted almost entirely for England, until the Civil War when shipping was stopped and the English textile industry found itself in a crisis. To meet this, the British began to produce cotton in their colonies, primarily India and Egypt, where Colonial management was a success. English cotton mills began to turn out many thousand times more cloth than they ever had. Indeed, there was so much cotton that English merchants could not sell it, principally owing to the fact that European countries as well as the United States, their chief customers, had themselves begun to make cloth in large quantities. India, Egypt and Japan where there were no modern factories became England's new customers.

In the United States there were enough raw materials and markets. Besides, chemists began to produce synthetic fibers which competed with natural materials. These synthetics, however, were made from a variety of materials every country has in abundance—air, water, coal, wood and limestone, so the new discoveries increased and, at the same time, complicated world manufacture and trade in textiles.

The discovery of synthetics had its origin in the invention of a new dyestuff in 1856 by William Henry Perkin, an Englishman. Perkin discovered a coal-tar dye to replace the vegetable matter which had been used from antiquity. The new dye was much cheaper than natural coloring. Soon after Perkin, German science and industry produced alizarin and other important synthetic dyes to satisfy worldwide demand. However, since the world wars, the United States has produced ever larger quantities of the total supply of artificial dyes.

The history of synthetic fibers, which

THE ART AND CRAFT OF HAND WEAVING

Fig. 31. Simple power loom (old type), Lowell, Massachusetts. Harness holds and lifts four shafts. Rod, at right, attached to beater, is mechanically driven. *Smithsonian Institution.*

began toward the middle of the nineteenth century, parallels the development of the dyes with which they were associated. The first step in synthetic fiber-making converted plant cellulose into a liquid, imitating the silkworm's process with its food, the mulberry leaf. Then, later, a machine was developed that turned liquid wood pulp into thread by forcing, or extruding, it through fine tubes. The first public appearance of a man-made fiber, artificial silk, was at the Paris Exposition of 1899.

Practical manufacture of artificial fibers did not begin until after the first world war, when vast supplies of cellulose and chemicals were available. These were converted into the new product, "rayon." This material, at first, was unpopular on account of its glossy finish and the fact that it tore easily when wet. Chemists subsequently perfected rayon in appearance and strength, so that now it is bought more often than wool and silk. It is an entirely practical, much-used fiber.

On account of the success of rayon, other synthetics soon appeared. The new fibers—nylon, orlon, saran, dynel and others—are not intended to replace natural fibers. They have new and different uses, and many of the synthetic fibers have qualities not found in natural fibers. Perhaps none of them, however, will replace rayon, just as rayon has not altogether taken the place of silk.

Loom Parts and their Function

The loom is the cloth-weaving instrument and ranges from the simplest wooden frame to the most intricate power-driven apparatus of modern industry. The purpose of the loom is to interlace yarns or threads by running one lot lengthwise in the loom, the other crosswise. The lengthwise yarns are called the warp, the crosswise are the weft, or filling. The two groups of threads, warp and weft, are interlaced at right angles.

Contemporary hand looms are of every size from small looms for tables, to large floor looms. The principal parts of hand and power looms are the same. They differ in size, in the materials of which they are made, as well as in style. Hand looms are commonly made of wood, birch, maple or walnut; power looms, of steel.

The outer frame of the illustrated loom chosen as an example (*Figs.* 32, 33, 34) consists of four upright posts connected by straight beams, forming a blocklike structure. It will weave a 38-inch material. In back of the loom is a large roller as wide as the loom. On this warp beam the warp yarns are arranged side by side and are as long as the cloth is intended to be. They are wound on the warp beam from the roller upwards and over a cross bar or back beam, toward the framelike shafts hanging in the center of the loom.

The harnesses or shafts hang from a superstructure built on the loom. Each shaft is an elongated frame with upper and lower strips of wood, connected at the sides by narrow metal strips. The pendant heddles are strung in an unbroken row of vertical wires on two rods, fixed at top and bottom inside the frame.

Fig. 32. Twenty-inch floor loom, four shafts. The parts are explained in diagram, *Fig. 33.* *Photo, David Vestal.*

The line-up of vertical strips, which cuts off the weaver's view through the loom, may be made of string, wire or metal. Each wire heddle has a loop, at top and bottom, which fastens to the horizontal metal strips inside

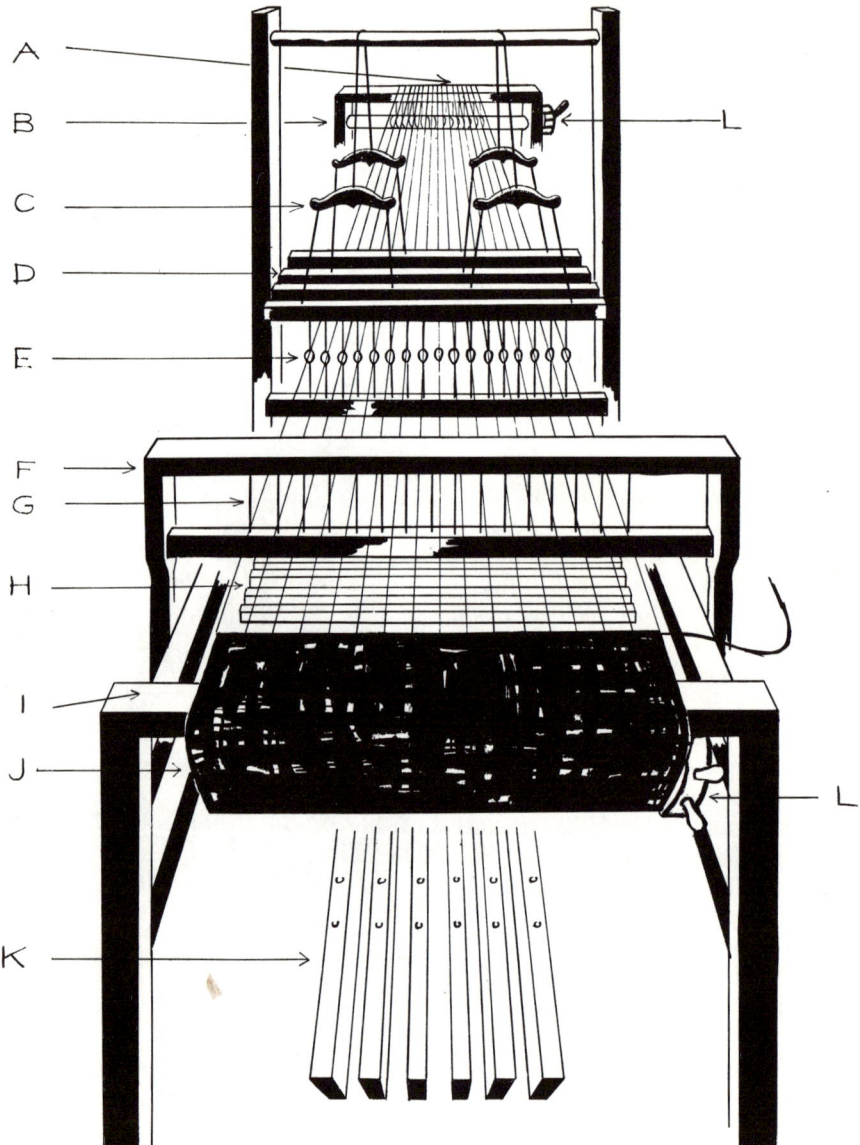

Fig. 33. Front view diagram of four-shaft floor loom.

A. Back beam
B. Warp beam
C. Heddle horses
D. Shafts, or harnesses
E. Heddles
F. Beater
G. Reed
H. Lams
I. Breast beam
J. Cloth beam
K. Treadles
L. Ratchet wheels

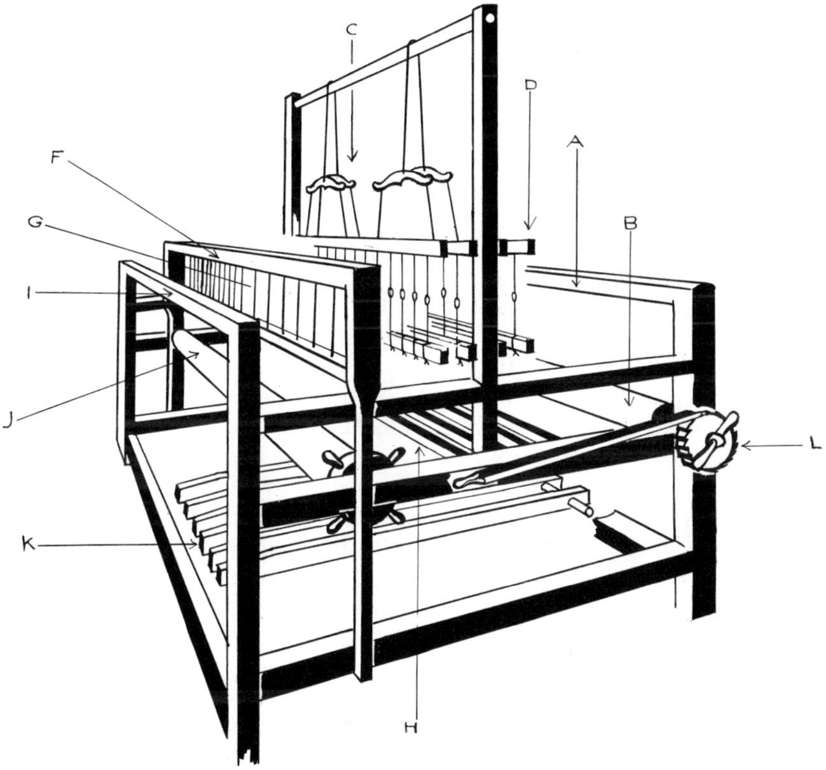

LOOM PARTS AND THEIR FUNCTION

Fig. 34. Side view diagram of four-shaft floor loom.

A. Back beam
B. Warp beam
C. Heddle horses
D. Shafts, or harnesses
F. Beater
G. Reed
H. Lams
I. Breast beam
J. Cloth beam
K. Treadles
L. Ratchet wheel

the frame. In the center of each heddle is an opening or heddle eye, comparable to the eye of a needle, through which each warp yarn is threaded.

On the illustrated loom are four shafts or frames each loaded with heddles through which are drawn, in succession, all the warp yarns the weaver will use. One thread through the heddle eye on the first shaft, the next through the heddle eye on the second shaft, the third on the third shaft and the fourth on the last frame (*Fig. 35*).

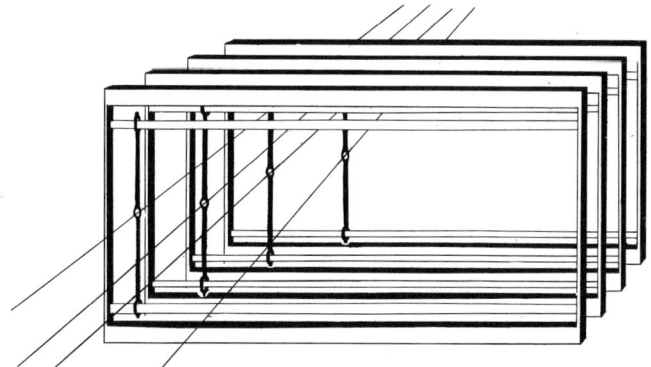

Fig. 35. Four shafts threaded with four warp yarns.

The shafts can be lifted in groups, or individually, depending on which warp yarns should be raised to make the desired weave.

On this loom, the shafts are fastened with hooks and short cords to heddle horses which adjust each shaft. The heddle horses resemble small coat hangers. A design's required number of shafts are hung from a series of these heddle horses, suspended but clearing each other. Each shaft is string-tied to heddle horses, joined by strings running over the pulley or superstructure, under the top crossbeam.

Immediately in front of the shafts is a long swinging frame, its uprights screwed to the bottom of the loom. The frame, wide as the loom, encloses a comb or reed. The warp yarns pass from the heddle eyes through the comb openings or dents. The function of the reed is to hold the warp yarns in place and at equal distance from each other. The reed governs the density of the warp threads after they have been put through the heddle eyes. If groups of ten threaded warp yarns (*Fig. 36*) are equally spaced, one inch wide, a reed of ten openings, or dents per inch will be the spacing required. It is also possible to put two threads through a dent, to get twenty threads per inch or a closer warp set.

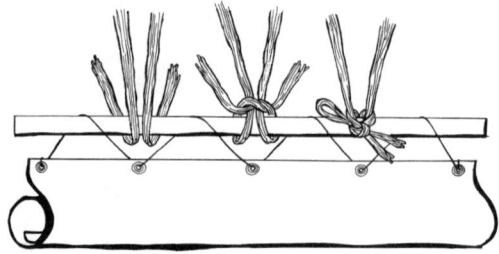

Fig. 37. Action of group tying of warp around rod.

The dented warp yarns go directly from the reed to the top of the breast beam where they are group-tied around a rod connecting with the cloth beam by cord or other sturdy fabric, called apron (*Fig.* 37). The breast beam is a cross bar in front of the loom. Its height is level with the heddle eyes, so that the warp runs straight to the front of the loom. The cloth beam is below the breast beam. The material is wound on the cloth beam as it is woven.

For the weaving action, or shaft lifting, the floor loom has treadles—long, flat pieces of wood attached to the cross beam at floor level, under either cloth or warp beam. Beneath the harnesses, at the center of the loom, are four long wooden rods, attached at the right to the frame of the loom. The wooden rods, lams, are the connecting link between shaft and treadle. A rod, or stick, is put through one end of the lams, so that they move freely. Strings or narrow chains are used to fasten the individual shafts to the lams and the lams to the treadles. Each shaft is tied to a lam. A ring screw is put in the center, underneath the front shaft. A long string is looped through the ring, passed down to the first lam, and connected. Shafts two, three and four are likewise joined to their respective lams.

The lams are fastened in a similar way to the treadles (*Fig.* 38). If shaft one and three should go down, they are connected by a string with a treadle. A string or chain is tied from the first lam to the first treadle and

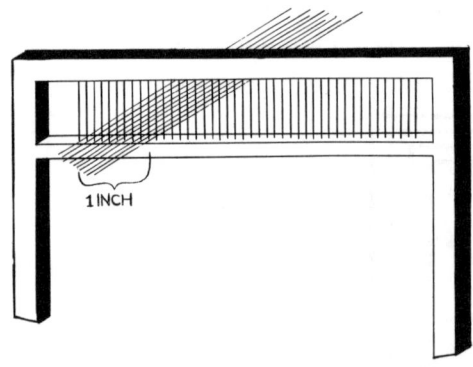

Fig. 36. Reed, in beater, with unit of ten dented warp yarns.

LOOM PARTS AND THEIR FUNCTION

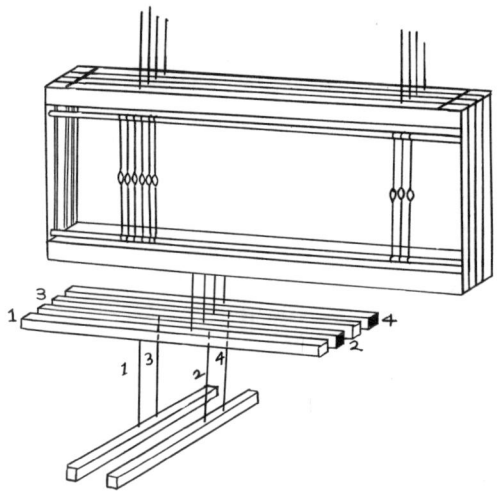

Fig. 38. Shafts, lams, and treadle connection.

another from the third lam down to the same treadle. When the weaver pushes his treadle, the front and third shafts lower and the others remain stationary. This operation forms a division or shed in the warp (*Fig. 39*). To achieve simple weaving, alternating shafts two and four have to be connected to the second treadle, as the first with the third.

The weaving area is the space at the front of the loom between beater and breast beam. The beater, or elongated swinging frame enclosing the reed, is moved back and forth.

Fig. 39. Divided warp shed and weaving area. Shuttle is thrown through shed.

The function of the beater is to push the wefts together after they have been put through the divided warp or shed.

After a few inches of weft are interlaced, warp from the roller is brought forward by means of a ratchet wheel on the outside of the right side of the loom frame at the end of the warp beam. A long stick, or pawl, screwed to the frame between the cloth beam and beater, fits into the pegs or teeth of the wheel. By pressing down on this stick, the weaver gradually advances the warp yarns. A hand-turned wheel, on the right end of the cloth beam, is used for winding finished cloth. The ratchet wheels on warp and cloth rollers serve to maintain even warp tension throughout the weaving process.

The function of looms is twofold. First, a loom must hold the lengthwise yarns or warp in tension in such a way that groups of threads may be raised and lowered to accommodate passage of the weft. The loom must, therefore, have heddle shafts or warp-lifting devices. The other parts—reed, treadles, and the like—make weaving easier and speed production. The basic loom has never changed but parts and improvements have been added for ease and speed.

Names of Loom Parts

WARP BEAM—At back of loom on which the warp is wound.

BACK BEAM—Bar at back of loom over which warp passes from warp beam.

HARNESS—Heddle frames, or shafts, hanging from top bar and attached below to lams and treadles.

HEDDLE—Needle of string, wire or metal, with eye or opening in the center.

LAM—Horizontal bar between heddle frame and treadle used to keep the heddle frames balanced.

TREADLE—Foot pedal used either singly or two at a time, according to loom. The heddle frames are raised or lowered, the warp threads drawn half up and half down to form an opening or shed in the warp, through which the weft is passed to weave the material.

BEATER—Cross-loom piece that holds the reed. It is used to beat the weft into place after it is put through the shed of warp yarns.

REED—Comblike part of the beater, made of metal.

DENT—Slit or opening between the metal teeth of the reed. The number of slits in one inch determines the number of threads to the inch in woven material. Warp threads are sleyed (drawn) through dents according to required density.

CLOTH BEAM—In front of loom. Material winds on this beam.

BREAST BEAM—Bar at front of loom over which the woven fabric passes before it winds on the cloth beam.

RATCHET—Wheel at end of warp and cloth beams to facilitate winding.

APRON—Heavy cloth fastened on back and front beam. The end of the cloth is connected with a long stick, around which warp yarns are tied.

Kinds of Looms and Tools

The width of looms varies from 8-inch table models to 80-inch floor looms. A medium size—the 40-inch—is a large piece of furniture, made in different styles. Some are short in depth and there are folding models as well (*Figs.* 40, 41).

Fig. 40. Weaving on 40-inch floor loom. *Photo, Hughes Fawcett, Inc., New York.*

KINDS OF LOOMS AND TOOLS

Fig. 41. Twenty-inch floor loom.
Photo, David Vestal.

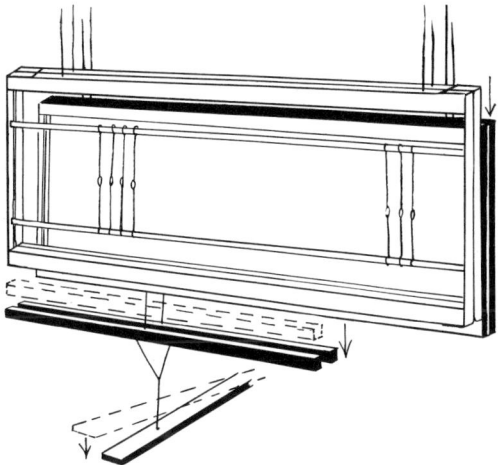

Fig. 42. Counterbalance system, in which shafts 3 and 4 (black) are lowered by pushing treadle connected with these shafts.

The choice of a loom depends, fundamentally, on the kind and width of material a weaver plans to make. Selection should also be guided by a little knowledge of varieties and kinds, so that a loom is bought which suits the weaver's taste. Choosing a loom is very much like deciding on a car or typewriter.

Counter-balance loom

Hand looms are manufactured with three different harness-lifting devices: counter-balance, jack-type and counter-marche. The counter-balance loom is simple to operate. If the weaver requires two shafts up and two down, he pushes the treadle with which the two down shafts are connected (*Fig.* 42).

But since counter-balance shafts operate tied in groups and by a pulley in the top of the frame, an uneven division of warp threads is hard to achieve. This limitation can be overcome with a little experience in adjusting the shafts or treadles. Irregular weave constructions can be produced on the counter-balanced loom.

Shaft and treadle hook-up of the counter-balance loom: If you have a pattern in which single shafts should be raised in succession, only the following connections are made. To one treadle, tie shafts 2, 3 and 4; to the next treadle, 3, 4 and 1; then, on the third, 4, 1 and 2; and on the last, or fourth, shaft tie 1, 2 and 3. Thus, with the first treadling, the first shaft is lifted. On the following, the remaining shafts come up, one after another. Using the counter-balance loom, you need to know only the shafts or warp threads meant to be down for a particular pattern.

Jack-type loom

On the jack-type, each shaft operates independently, permitting both balanced and unbalanced weaves. Jack-type looms operate exactly in reverse of the counter-balance. The treadles pull the shafts up instead of down—a result of the shaft-tying on top of the loom (*Fig.* 43). The mechanics are similar to those of a crane. When you need shaft one up, simply connect this shaft with one treadle.

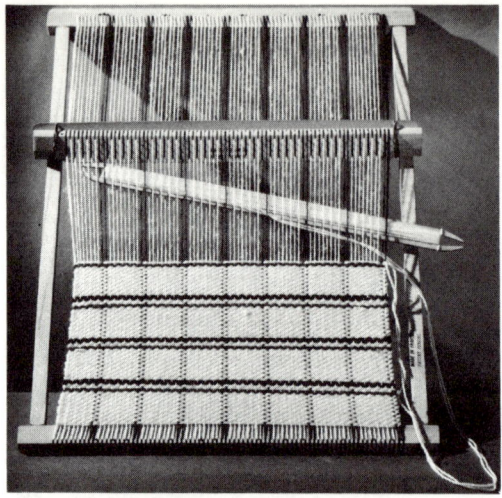

Fig. 44. Frame loom. *La Malle Tissanova Loom.*

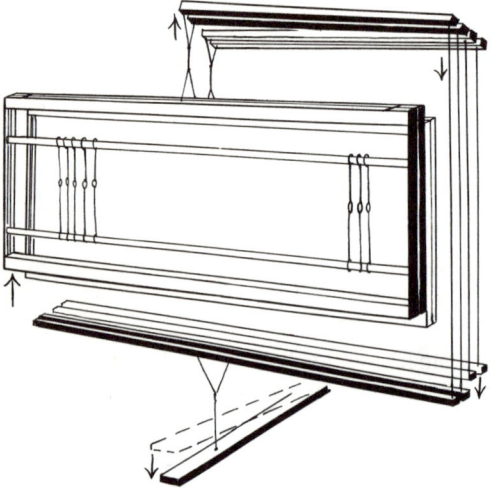

Fig. 43. Jack-type system. Shafts 1 and 2 (black) are raised by using treadle connected with these shafts.

Counter-marche loom

Counter-marche looms combine features of both the other types and provide for uneven weaves. But a double set of lams requires double tying. If the weaver wants shafts one and two raised, he connects two strings from the lams which raise the shafts and two strings from the lam set that lowers the other two shafts. Treadle action on the counter-marche is not so light as on the other looms, since all the shafts operate together in one movement.

Large looms are most useful and pleasant to work on, but smaller sizes have very many practical uses. On frame, or primitive looms, you can weave tapestries and learn a great deal about first principles. Small and primitive looms are cheap, too, ideal if one does not have space for large machinery. But on some small types there are no shafts, or beaters, and the weaving is slower than on treadle looms. Also, width and length of material are limited—as was the case in primitive weaving. Nevertheless, one can make enough yardage for a handbag or belt on frame looms. They are ideal for children and beginners.

Table looms, which are miniatures of the floor kinds, are popular among contemporary weavers. These make cloth 8 to 20 inches wide and have two to four heddle shafts and a beater. By beginning with a table loom the weaver conveniently learns fundamentals.

Loom choice

The majority of hand looms are in home use and reflect the twentieth century revival of interest in hand weaving. Most often it is in the home that men and women discover fabrics or develop their interest in a vocation and find a medium of art expression. A home

KINDS OF LOOMS AND TOOLS

Fig. 45. Table loom. *Photo loaned by Nellie B. Burow.*

loom should be as good as a commercial loom if weavers are to get encouraging results. If the home weaver has room, he will buy a good large loom. A 40- or 50-inch type with four shafts and six or eight treadles is practical. On this loom he can weave narrow and wide materials, suitings and large decorating fabrics. A well-constructed hardwood loom lasts longer than smaller, lighter styles. On a sturdy large model any weight of material may be constructed, even rugs.

A weaver can also choose a smaller floor loom—one about 20 inches wide. A considerable range of materials can be woven on this type—table mats, scarves and belts. Small looms are most inspiring and useful in inventive and experimental projects. Besides, one can always weave small, effective pieces and sew them together as jackets, upholstery and other useful and decorative fabrics.

Sometimes it is advisable first to buy a small loom in order to practice designing and become familiar with weaving.

The little table looms—least expensive of all—may be chosen because they are portable and as easy to put away as a typewriter or phonograph. They are useful, even if one owns a floor model, because on a table loom a designer may see his pattern and test it before setting it up in the large. For children, 8 to 12 years old, table looms are certainly the best educational choice.

Today, it is not infrequent for people to build their own looms, or have them built, according to specification. Blueprints for home construction are available, and weavers who have time and patience to make a loom find satisfaction in the product and the work it produces.

The choice of a loom for school or occupational therapy depends on budget, space accommodation and teaching objectives. Looms for occupational therapy are usually chosen or made for specific needs. In grade and high school workshops, one of each size and kind of loom should be represented. In school weaving, learning the uses of looms and becoming acquainted with yarns, color and weave is more important than yardage production. School looms should be good ones, in order to stand wear. Children and young people, beginning with frame looms, soon learn to use table and floor models. A wide variety of equipment is also commendable for art schools, vocational and therapy classes.

Warping frame

Besides a loom, the weaver needs other equipment, some of which he may make. Before the warp is arranged for threading through the heddles in the loom, he will need either a frame or a warping reel to hold the yarns in tight consecutive order and even length.

A warping frame is simple—almost exactly like a picture frame—and it is usually hung on a wall. The frame is furnished with

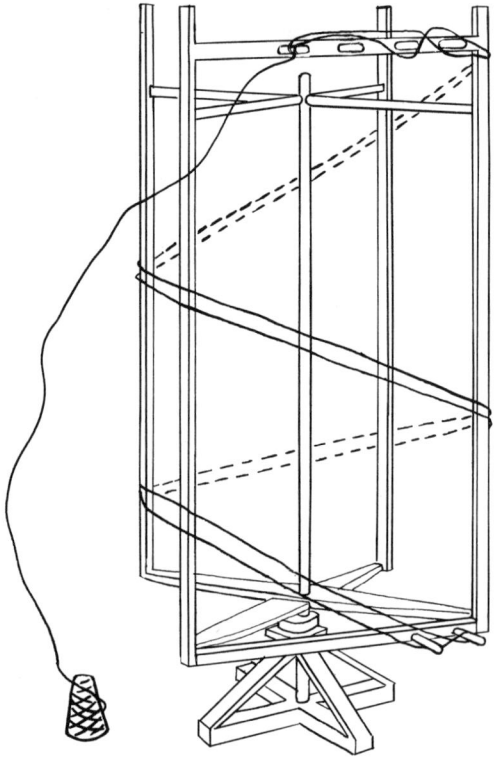

Fig. 47. Warping reel with wound-around arrangement of yarns.

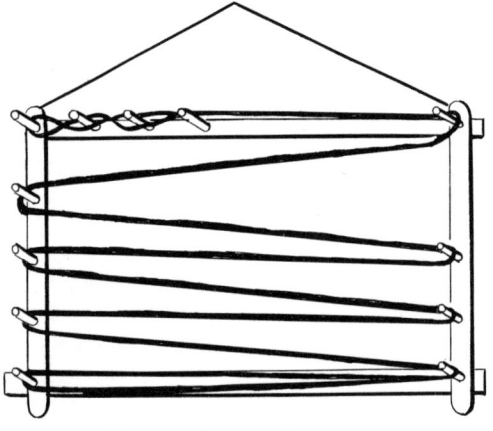

Fig. 46. Warping frame with yarns arranged crosswise.

pegs at intervals of about two inches, along top and sides. The weaver fastens the beginning of the yarn on the first peg at upper left. Then, the thread is guided across the frame and around the pegs, downward, until we have the desired warp length. The yarn is then led upward to the point where the end was fastened. This rotation is repeated until a desired number of continuous even lengths of thread are on the frame.

On small warping frames, 5-yard warps can be made; on large frames, 10-yard warps. Small warping frames are used only for narrow warps. Owing to their short pegs, they will hold very little. With fine yarns a weaver can sometimes make a 40-inch warp on his largest equipment. A medium frame, however, holds only small warps, about 5 to 10 yards long and sufficient thread to make a material 20 inches wide.

Warping reel

Although it takes up space, a reel is more conveniently used than a frame. The reel consists of two four-poster frames which revolve on a center spindle mounted in a base. Each side, from one upright bar to the other, is 27 inches across. The reel has removable cross bars which fit tightly between the uprights, however arranged or placed.

Reel operation is similar to frame warping. Put the cross bar with four pegs on top of the reel and fasten a yarn end around the first peg and arrange the warp cross. Turn the reel by hand, guiding the yarn around the frame to the length needed for the warp. One rotation of the reel may measure out three yards. The yarn is then taken back around the reel to the peg on which it was first fastened, and the reel is turned back and forth until the required amount of yarn for the warp is ready to lift to the loom. When not in use the reel can be taken apart and stored.

Spool rack

Yarn generally is bought on wood or fiber spools which can be slipped on the rods of a rack. The racks, which may be made or bought, hold 20 to 60 spools, but hardly more than 8 spools of yarn are required for a warp. A rack, like the one illustrated, a small upright frame equipped with a few movable horizontal rods, can easily be made at home.

Skein winder

For handling skein or hank yarns a winder is used. The illustrated winder, about four feet high, stands on the floor. It has an up-

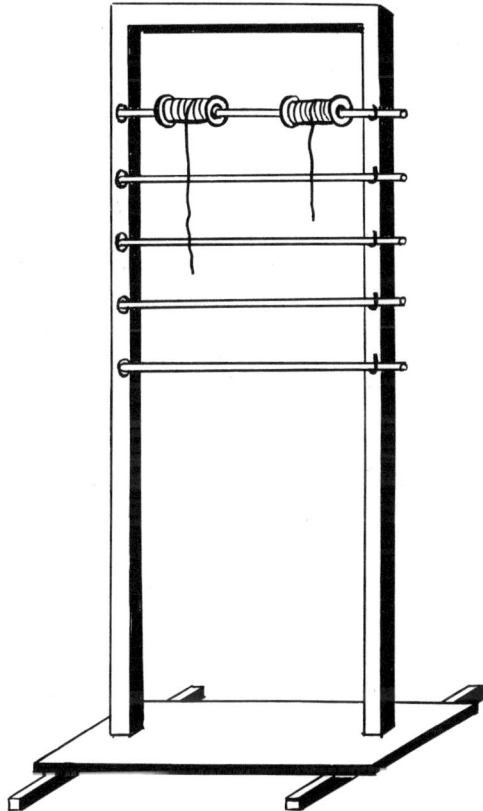

Fig. 48. Spool rack.

right beam with two movable rollers. The yarn is placed over the top and bottom rollers, which are adjusted according to the length of the skein. For the simple winding of yarn from the skein, a chair back may be used.

Bobbin winder

This tool is for making warp and filling spools. The bobbin winder in the illustration is screw-fitted to a table. It has a long spindle on which spools and weft quills fit tightly. The bobbin winder is generally used for winding yarn from a large spool, or skein, onto a small weft spool or quill.

THE ART AND CRAFT OF HAND WEAVING

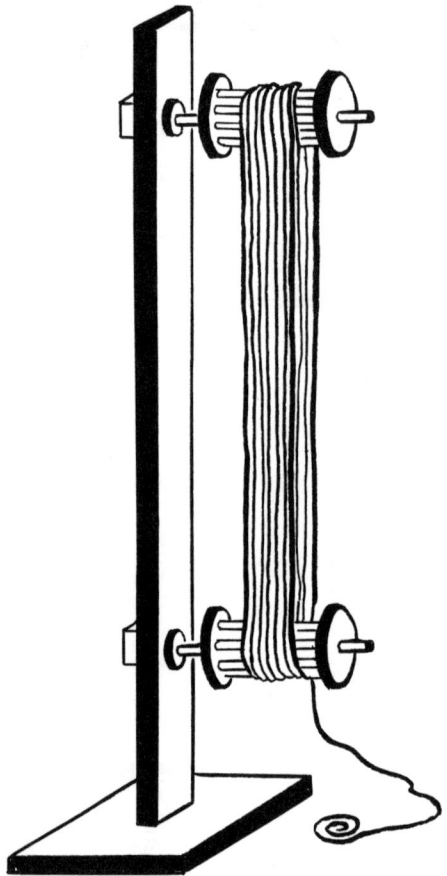

Fig. 49. Skein winder.

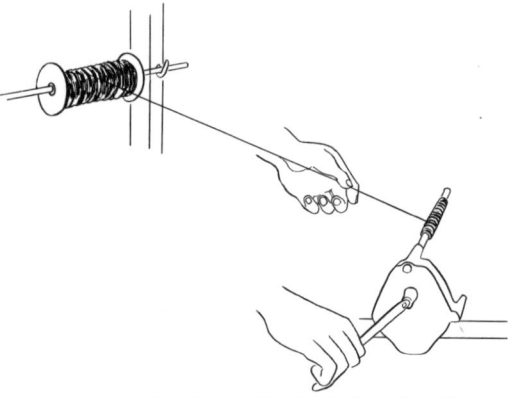

Fig. 50. Bobbin winder. Hand winding of weft yarn.

Lease sticks

Before the warp yarn is threaded through the heddle eyes on the loom it must be spread with a pair of lease sticks, either flat

Fig. 51. Lease sticks, used to separate and spread warp yarns in consecutive order across loom.

or round rods. These may be supplied with the loom but they can be bought at a lumber yard. Weavers also use the lease sticks instead of paper in the warp while winding or beaming it on the roller. Lease sticks of all sizes are used, but their length should equal the width of the loom.

Hooks

The yarns are drawn through heddle eyes and reed dents by means of a heddle or reed hook resembling a crocheting needle but long and flat and with a handle. The ordinary heddle hook (illustrated) can be used for both heddles and reed. However, there is a special reed hook that is shorter and wider than the one shown.

Fig. 52. Hook for threading heddles and reed.

Heddles

The heddles, which fit to the shafts, are of different styles and sizes. They are usually round, or flat, strips of metal, but they may be of wire or string. Some weavers prefer the string type because they slide noiselessly. Steel heddles, however, are much more convenient to handle during threading.

KINDS OF LOOMS AND TOOLS

The size or length of the heddles depends entirely on the height of the frames and shafts of the loom. It is always advisable to buy extra heddles since most looms do not come equipped with enough for practical use. String heddles may be made by hand on a heddle-making board, but this is tedious and takes time.

Reeds

Reeds are classified by the number of dents to the inch: A No. 10 reed, for example, has ten dents or openings per inch. The No. 10 can be used for various qualities, for instance: twenty ends per inch, with two threads to each dent. The choice of the reed always depends on the density of a projected fabric. The most useful reeds are Nos. 10, 15 and 20.

Shuttles

For weaving on small looms, flat fiber shuttles with the yarn wound on them are the only thing. These may be bought in sizes 6, 9, 12 and 15 inches long. For weaving on floor looms, boat shuttles—which are thrown from side to side—are generally used. The boat-shaped shuttle has a spindle across the top, fitted with a yarn bobbin or quill. The yarn from the bobbin is drawn through a hole in the outside of the shuttle. The style of the shuttle depends on personal preference as well as on the quality of yarn to be used, but customary shuttle length is 12 inches. Shuttles are made wide for coarse yarns, so that more material may be put on the bobbin.

Spools

Yarns are made up in different ways and quantities. The weaver, in preparing his warp threads, must often rewind the yarn from skeins to bobbins in order to make them easier to handle. Wood or fiber spools, about 4 inches long, are useful for this purpose. It is practical to buy yarn that is already on such spools.

The filling bobbins, or quills, used in the shuttle are about 2 or 3 inches long and of different shape from the yarn spools. The quill, which fits on the shuttle spindle, may be straight or tapered, of fiber, wood or plastic. Quills may also be homemade from brown wrapping paper, cut oval-shape, tightly wound and tape-sealed on the spindle of the bobbin winder.

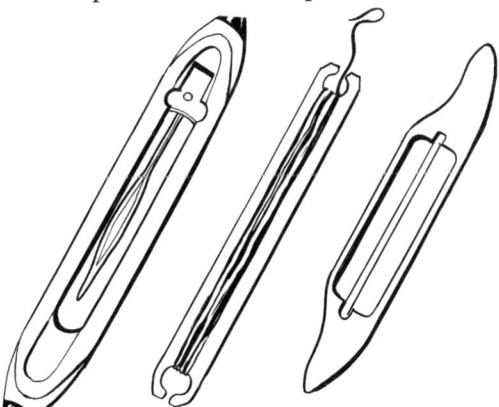

Fig. 53. Two boat shuttles and a flat shuttle (center) for small weaving.

Fig. 54. Weft bobbins, or quills, which fit in shuttle.

Weaving Procedure

Before he begins his project the weaver secures sufficient material for warp and weft. The weaver's yarns are made up in skeins, spools or cones, numbered according to a system (see Yarn Count) which tells us how many yards of thread are in one pound. From this we can calculate the exact yarn quantity for our materials.

Fig. 55. Yarn in skein, spool, and cone.

Warp preparation

Several steps that need not follow any fixed order are taken before the weaver makes the warp. He must determine density, that is, the number of warp threads he requires per inch. For an average tweed, he might use about 20 ends of warp threads. The weaver then determines the width of his material. The cloth in our demonstration will be 40 inches wide, therefore the warp will require 800 threads.

After we know how many threads are needed for the width, the length of the material must be decided. If we plan six yards of suiting, we must add some extra length for warp waste. The unwoven yarn ends are tied to the rollers at front and back of the loom. In addition to this unwoven warp, the length of unwoven warp in the areas in front of the reed and back of the harnesses must also be calculated. And since the warp will be in tension on the loom during weaving, allow for shrinkage of the material when it is taken off the loom. The size of the loom, the nature of the raw material and the weave construction are all factors that determine how much warp will be needed in addition to the finished material off the loom. An average of one to two yards of unwoven warp is the usual allowance.

Before unwinding spools of new yarn on the warping reel (*Fig.* 47), the weaver determines the number and length of the single threads he will prepare—in our case, 800 ends, 8 yards long. The weaver takes two spools and places them on the spool rack (*Fig.* 48). He stands with the warping reel at his left, the spool rack at right, and he ties the two yarn ends from the spools to the first peg on the upper crossbar of the reel. With the right hand, he separates and arranges the threads over the pegs to form a warping cross in order to keep the threads in consecutive order. The cross is formed between pegs three and four, alternating one thread at a time, over and under, between the two pegs (*Fig.* 56).

The weaver then revolves the reel and guides the threads around toward the right until the second cross bar and its two pegs are reached. The distance between top and bottom pegs is the desired warp length—8 yards. Two threads are now on the reel, each 8 yards long.

From the bottom pegs—where the yarns are guided together, over and under (*Fig.*

WEAVING PROCEDURE

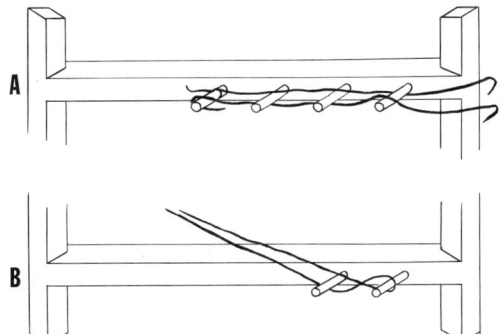

Fig. 56. Warping cross arrangements of yarns at beginning and end. A, top cross, beginning. B, bottom cross, end of warp.

47)—the weaver carries the yarns back up to the starting point while turning the reel in reverse. The first turn of two threads down and the return of two back to starting point provides four 8-yard warp threads or the beginning of the warp. The back-and-forth turning of the threads between the start-and-finish pegs on the reel is continued until the necessary 800 lengths of warp yarn are measured out.

When all the necessary warp is on the reel, the crossing yarns are secured between the pegs on the top and bottom cross bars with a long piece of yarn of different color from the warp (*Fig. 57*). The weaver begins with the top cross of yarn on pegs three and four, putting the tying yarn between the layers at peg four. He then draws the tying or security thread through the other division, along peg three, finally knotting the ends of the thread. The bottom cross is secured in the same way. When both crosses are tied, the warp is ready to be taken from the reel. The weaver removes the warp from top downward, winding it around his wrist to form the first loop, chaining off each thread, as in hand crocheting (*Fig. 58*).

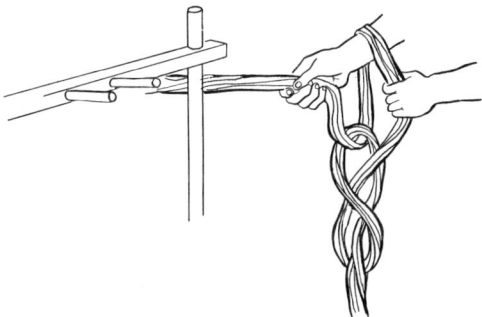

Fig. 58. Removing warp from reel.

Putting the warp on the loom

Beaming the warp is the action of putting, or winding, the warp on the back roller. The finished warp, which is a chain of yarn, must be evenly distributed along the roller to the width of the intended material. A tool called a raddle (*Fig. 59*) is used for this. The raddle resembles a coarse comb with a lid. It is about as wide as the loom and has two dents, or openings, per inch.

The warp we want has 800 ends, consist-

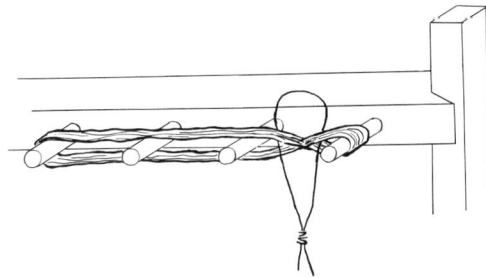

Fig. 57. Securing warping cross with a long thread.

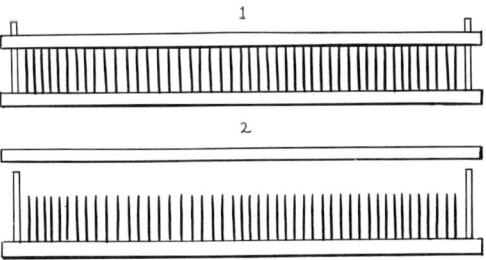

Fig. 59. Raddle. 1, closed. 2, with lid removed for distribution of warp yarns.

ing of 200 groups each, of the four yarns which led up and down from the two spools during reeling. Distribute these ends in the raddle comb to the planned width of the cloth—40 inches. Put ten threads through each dent, and continue distribution across the raddle: 40 ends every two inches.

The work of putting the threads in the dents of the raddle can be done on a table, but in our example it is done with the raddle secured on the back beam above the roller.

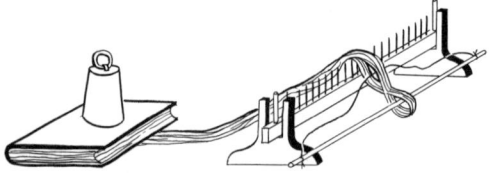

Fig. 60. Warp yarn distribution across raddle.

All the yarns are laid through the loom, over the shafts, with the ends hanging over the front and back beams. The two and two grouped cross (the bottom cross) hangs over the raddle on the back beam. When the warp is in the loom, replace the tying thread with a piece of string passed through the top division of the cross and tie to the ends of a stick that has been put through the lower division.

Yarn grouping in the raddle dents is done lightly, so that the long warp threads are not pulled and stay in position. After complete distribution—one dent, 10 yarns—a lid is put on the raddle to prevent the grouped yarns from falling out of the dents while beaming. The stick with the string, which holds the warp, is now fastened by means of four or five extension cords to the roller, or warp beam.

In order to wind the 40-inch warp on the roller perfectly, we clear out as much as possible of the shafting and interference at the center of the loom. The winding usually is done by two persons, one standing in front and one at the back of the loom. The person in front holds the warp ends tightly while the other turns the warping beam. The holder of the yarns must give them tension. He must not allow them to be pulled slackly through his hands. The person at the back turns the roller, and after some warp is on, puts between the warp layers sheets of paper which prevent the soft yarns from forming grooves or uneven tensions. For this 8-yard warp we use about five sheets of brown wrapping paper a little wider than the warp. The winding is continued until the end of the warp reaches the beam above the back roller.

The warp is then removed from the raddle and the security thread around the top cross is exchanged for two sticks—one put through one division of the yarn, and one through the other. Since the yarns are on the roller, they can be safely spread out, and the complete warp, with lease sticks, drawn forward to the heddle frames (*Fig. 61*).

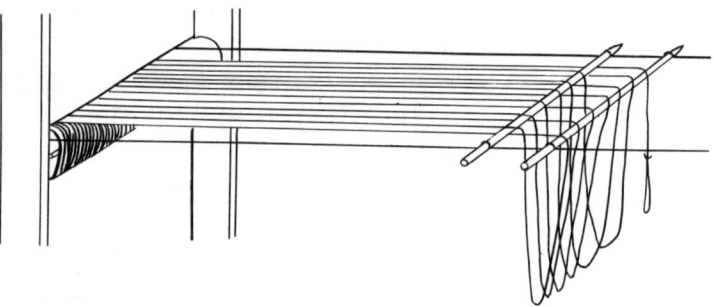

Fig. 61. Warp, with lease sticks, drawn forward toward heddles.

WEAVING PROCEDURE

The warp ends brought forward, near the heddles, are cut and tied in bunches, preparatory to threading.

Threading heddles

One after another the threads are drawn through the heddle eyes with an entering hook—a long, flat crocheting needle (*Fig. 62*). The weaver draws the first warp end by putting the hook through the first heddle eye on the first shaft. He takes the second yarn and threads it through the first heddle on the second shaft. Then the third thread is put through the first heddle eye on the third shaft, and the next yarn on the last, or fourth, frame—first heddle eye. This completes a threading unit of a straight draw threaded

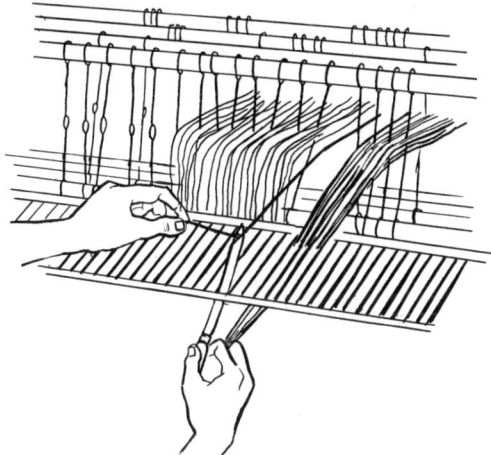

Fig. 63. Entering warp yarns, or sleying with reed down, removed from beater.

from front to back. We repeat the yarn threading until all the yarn ends are drawn through heddle eyes. After twenty or thirty are threaded, tie them for security.

When the entering process is done, put the warp yarns through the dents in the reed (*Fig. 63*). In this project of 20 ends per inch density, we use a 10-dent per inch reed. Two yarns will be put together through each dent or opening. Before taking yarns through the dents, pull the warp toward the front, so that the threads are long enough for easy handling. Begin the reed-entering, called sleying, with the first two threads, somewhat as in heddle-eye threading. Put the hook through the dent, grasp the first two yarns from shafts one and two and pull them through. Repeat, hooking the next two threads through the next dent. Continue until all yarns are dented. When finished, group-tie the threads so that they hang from the reed securely (*Fig. 64*).

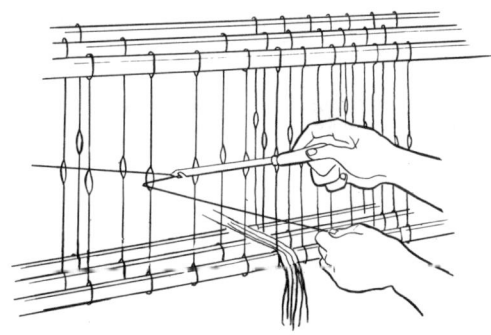

Fig. 62. Threading warp yarns through heddle eyes with hook.

Fig. 64. Reed with hanging groups of tied warp.

Tying the warp yarns

The group-tied warp threads, hanging in bunches from the reed in the front of the loom, have next to be secured to the rod that is connected to the cloth roller by cords or by a sturdy fabric apron. Before the warp-tying is begun, the weaver guides rod and extension cords, or aprons, around the roller and over the breast beam.

To tie the yarns, take the first small bunch on the left side, divide these in two parts and put them over and around the rod, fastening with knot and half bow. Next tie the bunch at the right outer side, and then the center group. The remaining, or intervening, yarn groups are knotted in this same fashion to the rod. And the yarns are straightened before they are tied to the rod, so that they will be level. The weaver tests for evenness and tension by going over the warp surface with his hand, and tightens the threads with the cloth roller ratchet. When all is satisfactory and evenly tensioned, he arranges the shafts for the pattern.

Shaft and treadle tie-up

Connecting shafts and lams with treadles is done on the floor. The lams are fastened to the shaft cords, one after another, from front to back. The weaver always follows his draft of the warp lifting procedure for lam and treadle tie-up. In this plain weave example, mending style, connect lams 1 and 3 with one treadle and lams 2 and 4 with the second treadle. When treadle 1 is pushed down, shafts 2 and 4 are up; with the second treadle down, shafts 1 and 3 are raised.

Testing the loom

After the shafts have been tied to the proper treadles, the weaver tests his work. A few inches are woven in contrasting color to see clearly if everything is in order. Often one discovers from the sample that certain threads are loose or that warp threads are misplaced in the reed and must be corrected before the material is begun. The tie-up, or the right shaft-and-treadle connection, for the desired weave is also checked. When everything is satisfactory, the shuttles are prepared.

Preparing quills for shuttles

It is usual to ready a large number of bobbins for weft, or filling, in order not to be interrupted during weaving. The yarn is wound from large spools onto the quills, or bobbins, by means of a winder (*Fig. 65*). The amount of yarn to be wound on a quill depends on the size of the shuttle. Quills are tapered and should be wound tightly.

Fig. 65. Shuttle with bobbin ready for weaving.

When enough bobbins are prepared, you are ready to begin the material.

Weaving—inserting the weft

A few definite steps make up the operation known as weaving. First, the treadle—dictated by the design—is pushed down, creating the shed through which the shuttle is thrown across the width of the material. The weft is then firmly pressed into the warp yarns by moving the beater forward. Shed opening, weft insertion and beating are the primary motions. As soon as the woven cloth is near the beater, more warp has to be released from the roller. The weaver loosens the ratchet wheel attached to the back or warp beam, and turns the front or cloth beam to bring up the warp supply. The letting off motion, getting more warp, is done

Fig. 66. Power loom shuttle entering shed. *The Wool Bureau, New York.*

at regular intervals and becomes automatic. Care is taken to preserve an even degree of warp tension.

As the weaver throws the shuttle back and forth he examines the selvage. If he wants a firm edge he pulls the yarn when he catches the shuttle. Beating is done evenly, with the hand placed on the center of the beater. With practice one develops a feeling for amount of pressure to exert to produce different qualities of cloth, such as loose and open, or tight and close.

Sometimes warp threads break during weaving. A new thread has then to be tied to the end of the broken one and afterwards mended into the fabric. The weaver coordi-

Fig. 67. Cutting finished cloth.

nates treadling, throwing the shuttle, and beating, while he looks across the material. As soon as he sees a mistake, he stops weaving to adjust a loose thread or other fault.

When the required yardage is finished, the cloth is cut across the width (*Fig.* 67). Roll it off the cloth beam and put it on a table for inspection. Places in the weaving may have to be corrected and visible knots joined to the fabric by mending.

New woolens are usually washed after weaving in lukewarm, soapy water and steam pressed in order to give a firm and soft touch to the cloth and make it easy to cut and sew.

Glossary of Weaving Preparation

WARP LAYOUT—Width of cloth, number of ends per inch, and length of finished cloth, plus unused warp.

WARP YARN PREPARATION—A warp can be made from a single thread, or four to eight yarns together. These are wound on warping spools proportionate to the number of spools required.

WINDING—There are several ways of winding warp, depending on equipment: warping frame for short warps, warping reel for long, or it can be done directly from spool rack to a sectional warp beam.

DISTRIBUTING, ACCORDING TO WIDTH—Putting warp yarns through dents of the raddle. Yarns are distributed in sections across the raddle.

BEAMING—Putting warp on back roller.

THREADING—Warp yarns entered, or threaded, through heddle eyes.

SLEYING—Warp yarns guided through dents of reed.

TYING—Bunches of warp yarns tied around rod connected with cloth beam.

TIE-UP—Lam and treadle connection, according to weave.

SHUTTLE PREPARATION—Winding filling yarn on bobbins, or quills, which fit in shuttle.

WEAVING—Insertion of weft and beating, or pressing, the weft into the warp.

There are several ways of preparing a loom. Sometimes the beaming is done first, followed by threading the heddles and sleying the reed. Or, a weaver may begin by threading, followed with sleying and winding the warp on front roller, before final beaming on warp roller is done. Some weavers set up their looms from front to back. They first dent, or sley, afterwards threading heddles and then winding the warp directly on the back roller. For short warps, up to six yards, one should first thread and dent, ending with beaming the warp. But for longer warps and for special yarns, the way demonstrated earlier in this chapter with the raddle is ideal procedure.

Part II. Fibers

General Characteristics

HAIRLIKE SHORT units of cotton and fleece are the fibers most often spun into yarn. Silk is a longer and straighter filament. It needs only to be unwound from a cocoon, since it comes already spun by nature. In textiles, short as well as long filaments have specific characteristics. An individual fiber must have considerable strength or it will be impossible to turn it into a useful yarn. A cotton spun from long fibers is stronger than cotton spun from shorter units because the fibers can be twisted together more often. The fiber units must adhere to each other during spinning. When several units of rough wool have been twisted together they are difficult to pull apart. Silk and synthetics, as a rule, have smooth surfaces and less resistance. Other desirable properties in fibers are fineness, elasticity and porosity (for holding dye).

The more pliable a fiber, the more easily it turns around another fiber. Stiff fibers, excepting perhaps linen, are not adaptable to spinning. Fineness is desirable in yarn. Jute, for example, is a coarse vegetable material and can be used only in heavy grade projects. Porosity (or porosity capilarity) is the ability of a fiber to absorb dyes or bleach.

Finally, the raw material should be capable of withstanding the conditions of wear to which it will be subjected. For commercial use, fibers must be available in large quantities and supplied at more or less regular intervals. There are many vegetable fibers, for example, that have important properties for textiles but the supply is too uncertain and expensive to make practical commercial weaves.

The natural fibers are direct products of animal, vegetable and mineral sources. The synthetics are evolved yarns, containing, for example, a cellulose solution that can be shaped into fine artificial threads. The ordinary animal fibers are wool and silk. The important vegetable yarns are spun from flax, cotton, hemp and jute. Asbestos is the primary example of mineral fiber, and silicates are now commonly used in making "glass" thread. Among the evolved modern products—synthetic, as opposed to natural yarn—are rayon, nylon and plastic. All these fibers, natural as well as synthetic, are processed before they result in weavable yarn.

Natural Fibers

Wool

Processing the fleece of sheep is the most important yarn industry. The finest wool

Fig. 68. Merino stud ram, Australia. *The Wool Bureau, New York.*

comes from Spanish merino, English cheviot and Rambouillet sheep. Merino, most often bred in New Zealand, South Africa and Australia, is the most popular. Delaine sheep, United States merino, produce the best and strongest domestic wool but the finest comes from Australia, principal among sheep raising countries.

Shearing fleece, the first step in wool processing, is done in spring with an electric razorlike tool. The cut wool is shipped to warehouses and mills for classifying and grading, put in bins where buyers can select. Grading is done according to fineness and length of fiber. On grading depends whether the finished product will be used for rough or soft fabrics. There may be as many as fourteen qualities of wool in a single fleece. However, modern methods limit the grading to three. Wool is judged by its feel, or handling, to determine softness and fineness. An experienced sorter is guided not only by handling but knows the position on a fleece of the different qualities.

Wool, as it comes from the sheep, is dirty and greasy. It is usually scoured in a bath of soap and soda (*Fig.* 70). Burrs and other vegetable matter are removed chemically by carbonization.

Dyeing and blending follow cleaning (*Fig.*

FIBERS

Fig. 69. Sheep shearing. The Wool Bureau, N. Y.

Fig. 70. Wool scouring. Wool is fed into scouring tank, or bowl, from bin in background. Moving spikes force wool through cleaning solution. *The Wool Bureau, New York.*

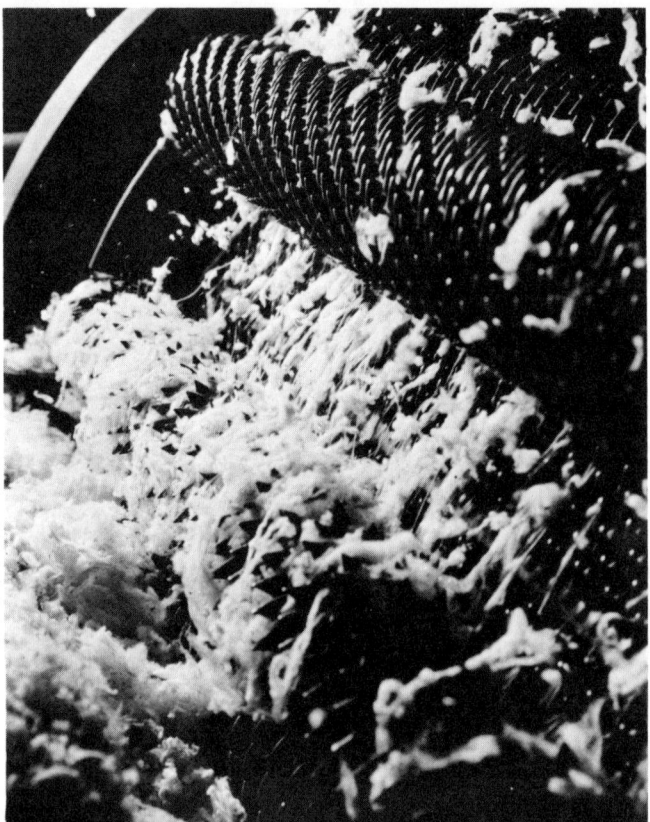

Fig. 71. Wool blending in mixing picker. *The Wool Bureau, New York.*

71). Stock-dyeing in this stage is the best process. No other yarn is dyed at so early a stage of processing. When the fibers come out of the dye they are evenly dried. A hydroextractor, similar to the kind used in large laundries, helps remove moisture. Then the wool is spread on a series of network frames, stacked one above the other, where hot air is fan-driven through the shelves. Drying is sometimes done in a large steam-heated chest, something like a storage refrigerator.

Blending wool is an important factor in this industry. Various kinds of wool—for example, Australian and Ohioan—are mixed. New wools in many shades may also be worked into attractive heather mixtures. This task requires ability—the knowledge gained by experience of what can be expected of different wools during carding, spinning, weaving and finishing processes. Frequent tests are made before the right combinations are reached.

Sheep fleece loses its oil after it is scoured and must be re-oiled to pass through succeeding processes. Oiling is done either by hand or by an automatic spray while the wool is spread on a floor, or as it passes on a belt to other machines. Short fiber, staple, wools are usually full of burrs, persistent in spite of the work of sorters and sorting machines. But the bits of vegetable matter must

FIBERS

be removed before carding or they will injure machinery and be crushed into the finished yarn.

Wool carding

Preparation for wool carding includes picking, teasing and opening fibers. Matted wool has to be disentangled, picked and straightened. Before the invention of the picking machine the process was done by hand. By machine the blended wool is put on a traveling belt that carries it into the teeth of a cylinder where the fibers are opened, mixed and made pliable. The material is then automatically passed to the carder.

Carding is customarily done by a set of three machines, much alike but for the gradation of teeth on the surface of the cylinders. In the United States the carders are called first, second and third breakers.

Wool carding is as old as spinning. The first carders were the fingers of the men and women who raised the sheep. A device for aiding the hand was later made of wood or bone, shaped like outstretched fingers. This card was succeeded by a pair of pieces of flat wood covered with animal skin and equipped with teeth made of thorns.

Fig. 72. Web of carded wool as it first comes from the rollers. *The Wool Bureau, New York.*

The principle of carding by hand is similar to the machine work. In the mechanical process, each breaker, or card consists of large cylinders against which small workers and strippers revolve. Thousands of teeth clothe the surface of the cylinders, becoming finer on each succeeding breaker. The first card opens the wool into thin layers, or slivers, that are automatically shunted to the second breaker. From the second, the sheet is delivered to the third. Wide slivers of wool are fed diagonally over the machine belt by jarring or by oscillation. Finally, the filmy wool is produced in half-overlapping layers. The wool from the final breaker goes to the spinning frames where it is manufactured into yarn.

Wool and worsted spinning

One system in wool spinning produces coarse woolen yarn. A second, requiring more processes, creates smooth worsted. The woolen yarns are spun directly after carding. Soft and slightly twisted strands, or roving, are wound on spools and put on a mule or

Fig. 73. Front of spinning frame. From the spools of roving, or raw yarn, at top of machine, the downward passing thread is finally twisted, or turned, by the machinery and wound on spindles. *The Wool Bureau, New York.*

FIBERS

ring-spinning frame. Strands of the fiber are pulled into tight, small twists made by mule-spinning bobbins. If the material is not stock-dyed, the yarns are wound into skeins or hanks on a swift. The skeins are washed and put in a dye in which they are kept moving to get an even color. Woolen yarns are used for rough materials, such as tweed, blanketing and broadcloth.

The worsted variety of yarn is a result of combing wool slivers before twisting them into even, lustrous threads. A number of slivers are drawn out and the fibers arranged side by side in a process called gilling. After the slivers have been gilled, they are level and almost parallel. However, short and curly fibers are still mixed. Combing removes the short wool curls, noils, and makes the long fibers parallel, in a formation called tops. The tops are reduced to sizes small enough for spinning and then wound on bobbins.

The Bradford or English worsted system requires long, staple wool and creates smooth, lustrous yarn for suitings. French, or dry, spinning employs shorter, less oily wool and produces soft, dull yarns. The main difference between the methods is in drawing and spinning. The Bradford system uses much twisting, while the French worsted method does not. Winding is the process that follows immediately after spinning. The spools and skeins of yarn are then ready to weave, or, in some cases, ready for dyeing and plying.

Other hair fibers

Sheep provide the most important wool fiber but the hair of other animals is also useful in textile production. Specialty and luxury fibers are mohair from the Angora goat, Cashmere goats' wool, Peruvian llama and alpaca wool, vicuña and camel hair. One of the fine quality animal fibers is angora rabbit; the coarsest, perhaps, is horsehair.

Mohair

This material is produced from long and curly Angora goat fleece, with an average fiber length of 9 to 12 inches. Most of this fleece comes from Turkey, but Angora goats are also raised in Texas. Mohair, like sheep wool, is graded according to fineness of fiber. Kid mohair is the best. The white or brown fleece is cleaned and sometimes combed but carded only when it is combined with other fibers. The slivers of wool are spun by the worsted system.

Mohair is lustrous and superior in elasticity to sheep wool. It makes an ideal effect-yarn for upholstery. Its extreme elasticity prevents wrinkling, thus it is also a good yarn for tropical suitings, neckties, and the like. Another quality of mohair is its dyeing capacity. Colors show well in this fiber; and, owing to its natural luster, brilliant shades are especially effective.

Cashmere

This is a long-fleece goat fiber with glossy outer hair and a soft down of wool. The product is directly combed from the animal. Cashmere herds are raised in Tibet and surrounding districts. Mohair and cashmere are similar in their definite luster and elasticity.

The amount of yarn that Cashmere goats yield is small, therefore the fiber is expensive. Usually it is mixed with other wools, which makes for strong fabrics and clothes that hold shape.

Llama, alpaca, and vicuña

Llamas and alpacas are small, humpless, camel-like animals of South America. Alpacas usually are brown, but a few shade from white to black. The fibers of their wool are long, similar to Angora mohair. Alpaca cannot be bleached, therefore it takes dark dye only. This is an advantage—alpaca can be combined with light fibers of other materials, and the whole dyed without affecting the dark alpaca color, characteristically brown. Llama wool is lighter, coarser, and shorter than alpaca—otherwise, they are closely related materials.

The finest and softest South American wool is from the vicuña, a wild animal that is hunted, killed, and skinned for this purpose. The color of the vicuña is light brown. This is probably the most expensive wool and very high prices are paid for cloth woven from the yarn.

Camel hair

Camel hair is a vibrant tan color, usually, and has good textile qualities. The center of supply is Mongolia. The fibers, shed by the animal in heavy layers, comprise an inner and outer coating containing fine as well as coarse hair. The best comes from the underside of the layers of wool and, as a rule, is combined with other wool fibers. Camel hair is an insulator, therefore a yarn highly valued for winter coat and blanket materials. The supply never exceeds the demand, thus so-called camel hair is almost always a mixed product.

Rabbit wool

Soft, fluffy and light, this slippery material usually has to be combined with other fibers. Rabbit hair blends make soft, beautiful yarn creations.

Silk

Silk is the precious material of the textile industry. Its favorable qualities were prized in antiquity: its intense lustre, strength, softness, and elasticity. We enjoy satins and shantungs, which, being made of silk yarn, exceed all other fabrics in brilliance.

There is no certainty when the Chinese discovered that the moth larva spun good thread. The discovery was a guarded secret until the fifth century, when the Japanese learned about it and brought silk into history. Emperor Justinian, in the sixth century, is believed to have smuggled out of China the worms that introduced silk to Europe. The use of silk reached its peak during the Renaissance. Today Italy is the third largest producer.

The processes in silk production are sericulture, worm-raising and selling of cocoons; reeling, unwinding cocoon silk into skeins; and throwing, the twisting together of two or more filaments. Silk yarns are two kinds—wild and cultivated.

Sericulture

Mulberry tree and silkworm cultivation require infinite patience and favorable climate. The silk moth evolves in a short time from egg to worm to chrysalis to adult moth. Masses of worms are collected on sheets, washed in cold water, kept a few days in damp atmosphere, and put in cold storage. Here they remain until the young mulberry leaves are out and the time has come to incubate a season's batch of worms. The hatched silkworm is of hairlike thinness and about one eighth of an inch long. But the worm eats fifty times its weight and matures to be about three inches long.

The mulberry leaves on which they feed are chosen with particular care, since the quality of silk depends on the leaves. When the worm is ready to spin, he begins with a movement of the head, as if making a figure eight. Glutinous filaments consisting of silk fiber and sericin are ejected from two openings under the mouth, which harden into one fiber as soon as they hit the air. When the silk is exhausted, the worm changes into a chrysalis, then into a moth, which moistens the end of its cocoon of silk and breaks its

FIBERS 53

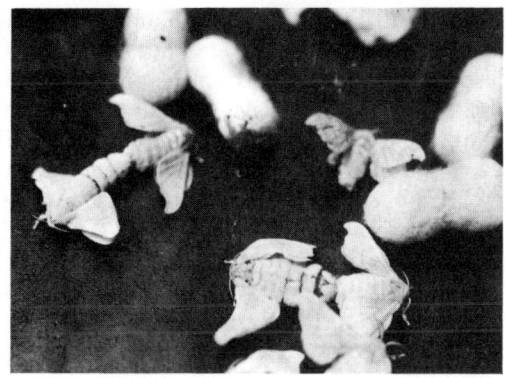

Fig. 74. Silk moths coming out of cocoons. *National Federation of Textiles, Inc., New York.*

way out. For the production of raw silk, the chrysalis is killed by heat, so that the moth cannot develop and destroy the silk. For reproduction purposes some moths are allowed to emerge, and the wasted cocoon provides material for spun yarn.

Reeling

Cocoons of raw silk, ready for unwinding, are sorted by color, shape and condition. In its natural state, silk is bright yellow, but scouring changes the yellow to pure white. Cocoons are soaked in hot water to soften and remove some of the gum, or sericin. A reeler takes the cocoons from the basins, removes the first loose silk, which is waste. (*Fig. 75*). Then he takes the good silk from several cocoons and reels it into a skein. The thread from one cocoon measures from two to six thousand yards. The number of fibers

Fig. 75. Silk reeling, Japan. *National Federation of Textiles, Inc., New York.*

composing the strand, however, is not the same at all points. An individual filament varies in thickness, therefore some parts contain more threads than others, in order to produce a single yarn that is even throughout its length. The reeled silk is now ready for throwing or twisting.

Throwing

In twisting silk fibers into continuous yarn, several cocoons are combined and turned into various qualities of thread. Organzine and tram are the principal types. Perfect cocoons are selected for organzine, which consists of a single thread twisted to the left and two or more to the right. Organzine twist which is the finest quality of all, has 16 turns per inch in a single yarn and 14 for the doubling. Tram silk, which is from a lower grade of cocoon, is a few single threads twisted together by only a few turns.

Other descriptions of silk yarn are chiffon and crepe twists. Chiffon is a single twist of 30 to 75 turns per inch; crepe twist has 2 to 15 threads, turned 40 to 90 times per inch, as a rule.

Spun silk

Unlike thrown silk, which is reeled and later put through twisting processes, spun silk may be spun artificially. The long filaments from cocoons are broken into short fibers and twisted the same as wool yarn. Schappe and bourette are major grades of spun silk. Schappe is waste, or residue, undesirable for tram and organzine. The waste from schappe is processed again into an even coarser yarn—bourette.

Silk qualities and uses

Silk yarns are named after the country of their origin. Asiatic silks are known as Chinese and Japanese filature and have special characteristics of manufacture. Some of the Eastern silk is uneven and slubby, giving a streaked effect when woven. These materials also vary in natural color from yellow to white. Japanese silk is soft and has little gum, or sericin. The Chinese is a very good warp yarn with a hard gum content which can be boiled off, producing the softest quality of silk in the world.

Wild silk, from worms fed on oak leaves, produces the irregular tussah yarn used in shantung. Douppioni, an Italian shantung thread, is processed when two worms, while spinning, get their filaments tangled. Japanese and Italian sericulturists produce this coarse but effective design yarn.

Cotton

Cotton is the seed fiber that provides most of the cloth produced in the world. The principal cotton growing countries are the United States and India. Cotton is a shrub, three to six feet high, with yellow or white flowers, depending on the species. The blossoms develop into a fruit, or boll, which contains seeds imbedded in the fibers used for yarn.

The type of cotton known as Sea Island, the finest quality, is grown in the Southern United States, West Indies, Egypt and Peru. Upland cotton, another important grade, has shorter and coarser fibers than Sea Island. Upland cotton is grown in the United States and other parts of the world. The strongest is spun from the cream-colored fiber produced in Egypt.

Planting and picking

The cotton-planting season in the United States is from March to mid-May. In Egypt it is from early March to the end of April. When the earth is warm enough for germination, and danger of frost is past, seeds are planted. Eight to twelve days later the young plant pierces the soil. Before it reaches full height, the plant forms stalks which blossom

FIBERS

Fig. 76. Picking cotton. National Cotton Council of America, New York.

in approximately a month. When first opening, the flowers are yellowish white, but slowly change to pink or reddish hue, and in about three days are shed. Fertilization occurs before the blossoms fall. The seeds, or ovules, grow rapidly and the plant reaches maturity, or ripe, open boll in about four months. Fine, long-fibered cotton, however, requires more growing time.

Picking is usually done by hand. Men, women, and children work long days in the field, and picking has not been successfully mechanized. The picker must discriminate between ripe and unripe, take hold of the fibers inside the boll, and reject the leaves of the plant, while leaving certain parts of the boll on the shrub.

Ginning

The first step in preparing raw cotton for spinning is ginning. Ginning cleans and separates the fiber from the seeds and lint substances. In early processing, cotton remains unrefined, but grades of cotton always depend on careful ginning as well as skillful picking.

Two kinds of traditional gins are used: the

Fig. 77. Cotton ginning. *National Cotton Council of America, New York.*

saw (invented by Eli Whitney, 1793) and the roller, of India. A recent machine, however, cleans as much as four thousand pounds a day. This gin has circular saws (forty to eighty on a shaft) which project through a slotted plate. Raw cotton is carried against the saws, which separate the fiber mass from the seeds which fall into a container below the gin.

The cotton remains somewhat entangled and full of dirt after ginning when it is baled for the mills.

Classifying and grading

Cotton is priced according to trade standards of grade and color. Fibers of the highest spinning value are generally the cleanest. However, the main point in judging is by fiber length, called staple. Long-staple cotton measures $1\frac{1}{8}$ inches per fiber. Shorter than that is graded as short fiber.

The characteristics of cotton—strength, uniformity, smoothness or silkiness—are also values for grading. The uniformity of fiber lengths, or the degree of mixture of staples in a consignment is an important factor. Besides, cotton may be weather-stained or immature. A cotton buyer, in addition, must consider the use to which he intends to put the material.

FIBERS

Fig. 78. Cotton lap, rolled sheets of fiber. *National Cotton Council of America, New York.*

Spinning

The purpose of cotton spinning is to twist cleaned fibers that are parallel, carded and evenly combed, into yarn.

When the tightly packed cotton bales are opened, the masses of fiber are carried on a traveling belt to a breaker, a machine which opens and mixes the fibers of various cottons of the same length. Then it is carried to machine pickers to open the cotton still wider so that sand, cotton neps or specks, leaves and dust may be entirely eliminated and form the mass into an even lap. The lap (*Fig.* 78) is a sheet of loose fibers somewhat like the cotton batting used for medical purposes.

Each step develops the raw material. Fibers become cleaner, softer and more parallel. The film is finally rolled into a wide lap, ready for the carder.

The card is similar to the one used for wool. Flat bars with teeth are fastened on a continuous chain that passes over a cylinder which also has teeth. Here the last neps as well as poor fiber are finally separated from the good cotton. When it is completely carded, the thin veil of material is taken off the cylinder and reduced to a narrow sliver

THE ART AND CRAFT OF HAND WEAVING

Fig. 79. Veil of cotton fiber drawn into sliver, at left. *National Cotton Council of America, New York.*

by being passed through an eye between rollers.

Cotton is combed when fine grades of yarn are wanted. Small slivers from the card are united by machine and fed to the comber, which extracts short ends and impurities. Selected fibers of even length are laid parallel and overlapping, forming larger, ropelike slivers. The combing processes are repeated until the slivers grow very silky.

Drawing and doubling

Again several slivers of cotton are united and drawn to make a smooth single sliver. From four to eight of these are combined and drawn together by rollers. Here, by drawing, they are reduced in size and then twisted into yarns, which are later wound on bobbins and made ready for spinning.

Cotton spinning is done on ring frames. The roving (*Fig.* 80) is drawn out by sets of rollers to the extent desired in a weaving work, then twisted and wound on bobbins. Warp yarns are more tightly twisted than threads used in filling. A great deal of weaving is done with single-twist yarns, but there are also many projects that require combinations or plies of thread.

Cotton yarns are treated in various ways

Fig. 80. Cotton sliver, or roving, ready for spinning. *National Cotton Council of America, New York.*

to enhance or disguise their natural qualities. Where maximum strength and luster are desired, tensed cotton yarn is mercerized, that is, treated in a solution of caustic soda. And, for certain uses, yarns are coated with rubber or plastic solutions. As for color, cotton is usually dyed in the yarn, not in the unspun state, as in wool.

Linen and other bast fibers

These materials grow between the bark and woody part of plants and are stiff. They have neither the pliability nor the smooth construction of cotton or wool. Bast fibers, as a group, have many similarities, although each has its distinguishing qualities. Linen, for example, is the most finely grained. Textiles made of it are always lint-free and easy to clean. Hemp, however, is one of the coarsest fibers. It bleaches well and is generally used in sack weaving. A related fiber, jute, also is coarse and takes dyes beautifully (in bright, pure colors, which soon fade), as seen in the burlaps woven from it.

Linen

Flax, a plant which was grown, processed, and spun in ancient Egypt, is the fiber of linen. Today flax is mostly cultivated in Belgium, Ireland and Germany. Oregon is the United States flax-growing center. Fibers are obtained from the plant with considerable difficulty. After the stems have been cut and decayed or retted, usually outdoors, the fiber is removed by breaking, scutching and hackling with knives to separate the filament from the woody core.

Two methods are practiced in flax retting. In one, the straws are soaked in clear, soft, running water for about two weeks, usually in crates placed in rivers and ponds. Another outdoor process is dew retting, in which the flax is spread in fields to ferment. The rapid method is by chemicals or steam, although this is not considered to be so satisfactory as outdoor retting.

After the flax has been retted and dried, the inner wood of the straws is split lengthwise. A simple stand machine with a series of long knives and beaters is used to crack the split wood into bits. Elaborate recent machinery has several pairs of grooved rollers through which the straw is passed. The pith is broken by the rollers, which expose and release the fibers. These are taken to the scutchers—a simple machine that beats and refines the flax pulp.

As the stalks are shaken and beaten to remove coarse pieces of wood or bark, the fiber begins to emerge and, in this stage,

Fig. 81. Raw flax, broken on tool at right, is swingled and combed to remove bark. *Smithsonian Institution.*

looks like gray hair mixed with straw. Flax once was cleaned and beaten on benches, or hung on a wall and swingled or beaten. Today scutching machines have a series of revolving wooden beaters that rapidly break off all short fibers, which are used for scutching tow, a coarse yarn. The long fibers are called line, or linen. The cleaned line, after scutching, is bundled and baled for market and for the spinning mills.

At the mills the flax is opened, again cleaned, and straightened for spinning. The rough flax is put through coarse combs that remove the last bits of tow and dirt, and finally is combed smooth by hackling machines.

Sorted line, used in fine yarns, consists of cleaned stems of fiber which usually are cut in three divisions, the center section producing the best yarn. Linen fibers are long. Bunches of them are run on a belt to a spreadboard where the thread-making process is begun by combing them with fine wires into continuous ribbons or slivers. The drawn slivers are doubled. Linen spinning frames are similar to those for wool and cotton. Several machines are required in the final processes, according to the quality of thread desired.

Both wet and dry spinning are used for flax. Wet spinning produces fine threads without much gloss. The dry-spun yarns have greater firmness and are used in good products. Preparation of linen yarn before weaving is the same as for other textiles. Sizing is used to strengthen warp yarns, which frequently are bleached before weaving.

Linen weaving requires an atmosphere in which the warp threads can be kept moist. The finishing of this material adds notably to its appearance. Usual finishes in an Irish mill are bleaching, starching, washing, beetling and calendering. The last finish is by hydraulic pressure.

Ramie

This bast is sometimes called china grass. It has many valuable properties, and, to a minor extent, is cultivated in the United States. India, Japan and South America, however, produce most of the supply.

The woody stalks are cut as they mature. Ramie bark, when green, is hand-stripped and scraped without retting. When it is dry it is dew- or water-retted, like hemp and flax. The fibers are sun-dried after they are rid of woody matter. Combing, drawing, and spinning follow. Ramie is more difficult to clean than flax and, until the gums in it are removed, it is coarse and rough. With degumming, the fiber becomes soft, white, and silky.

In fact, ramie is often combined with silk and is made into materials to compete with linen. It is as difficult as linen to dye. But it is strong and durable, and is used in such disparate weavings as fine lace and heavy canvas. It is popular in upholstery and other household decorative fabrics.

Jute

Jute generally is used in the cheaper grades of textiles. Its present use in decorative fabrics has increased its value. A bast fiber, jute must be retted and the filaments separated by hand. The plant grows in tropical India and in China.

Carpets, upholstery and burlap are made of both fine and coarse jute yarns. The yarns are effective and easy to dye, but they do not wear well and tend to fade.

Hemp

Kentucky and Italian hemp are perhaps the best known varieties. Dew-retting of the hemp plant was formerly the process used in the United States, but today the core is separated by machine. Hemp is yellowish gray, like linen. It is stout and bleaches well. Coarse hemps are used in canvas, carpet and rope making. Fine qualities are employed in fishnets and cordage. Textiles for contemporary home furnishing also use hemp.

Structural fibers

Unlike bast fibers, which are obtained from the stems of plants, the structural fibers are from leaves and fruits. These structural fibers, all of them tropical, usually are coarser, stiffer and less suitable for spinning than bast and seed fiber.

The large leaves of pineapple contain a filament that is usually extracted by hand and made into one of the most delicate vegetable products, pina. Cloth woven from pina is found at its most perfect in the Philippines where it often is combined with silk. Pina, besides being white, soft and lustrous, is also flexible and strong.

Manila hemp, a Philippine product made from hemp leaves, is more brittle than true bast hemp. The hemp leaves are cut before the plant flowers and are slit in order to remove layers of fiber which are scraped free of pulp and dried. The fibers are shaken, washed and spun. Sheer materials are made from finely beaten Manila hemp. The coarser varieties are used to make binding twine and heavy fabrics.

Sisal hemp and maguey, cultivated in the West Indies, Central America and Mexico, are of the agave family. The filaments are extracted from the leaves, and though the yarn is not strong, it is useful for commercial sacking and binding twine.

Kapok, a flossy, pod substance, is produced in the Philippines where it is transformed into light, elastic yarns. The pods are picked before they are quite ripe, so that the floss will not be spoiled by rain. The raw material is cleaned by hand and spun.

The fruit fiber of commercial importance is coconut, which is obtained from the covering of the fruit. Four to ten inches long, the hard, brown filaments are practical as rope and matting yarns.

Asbestos

This material comes from rock and is spun into yarn. It is fire- and acid-proof and deflects heat. Asbestos is used for theater curtains as well as in pads, iron holders and chemists' gloves where protection is necessary.

Synthetic Fibers

In the Middle Ages, the goal was to convert the ordinary into the precious; modern research elevated the artificial above the natural. Gradually, it has become evident that there is more profit in an article cheaply mass-produced in synthetic materials than in luxury goods of natural materials which few can afford. It has been proved that a demand for goods can be created where none existed so that a wholly new concept of production and merchandising has arisen. Entirely new textiles woven from synthetic fibers peculiar to the twentieth century are sold on their own particular merits.

The first man-made fiber, rayon, was designed to imitate silk. It was developed in Europe at the end of the nineteenth century, along with a host of other inventions that were to affect our lives. The first rayon factory in the United States was built in 1910. Although rayon has not replaced silk it has created a vital market of its own. The newer synthetics, such as nylon, orlon, dynel and others, are simply products of scientific research. It is not likely that any of these materials will replace rayon, just as rayon has never altogether taken the place of the natural fibers it imitates.

Artificial yarns are described or identified by their compounds. Regenerated cellulose fibers—viscose and acetate rayons—are made from either wood pulp or cotton linters, chemically treated and wet or dry spun. A second group—nylon, for example—is composed of mineral ingredients (carbon and hydrogen) drawn from air and water. Orlon, vinyon and saran are resin and plastic products.

Artificial yarns are made into long, continuous filaments, and, for special purposes, cut into short staples. The short threads can be made to look like wool, and some synthetics have qualities that are superior to natural materials. Of special interest is the fact that the diameters of synthetic filaments can be determined and thus permit greater variety in yarn creation.

Rayon

Viscose, cuprammonium and acetate are three of the rayon formulas. Most of the world's rayon yarns are viscose, made of wood pulp and cotton linters. These natural materials are transformed into cellulose sheets when treated with caustic soda. The

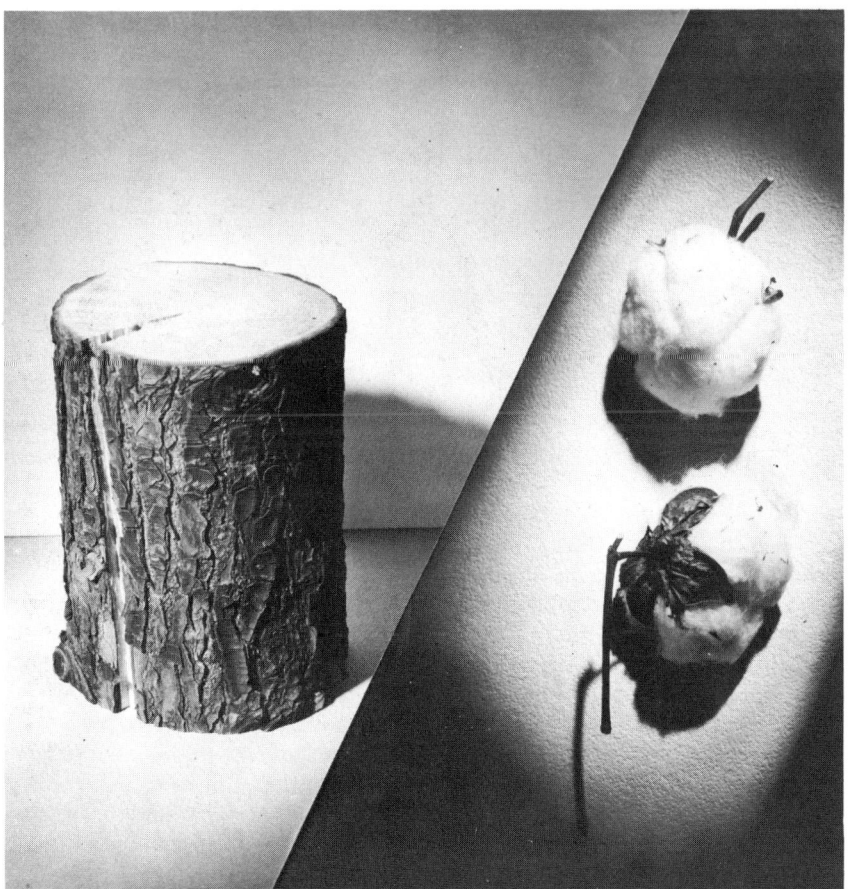

Fig. 82. Wood and cotton, source of cellulose, from which rayon is made. *American Viscose Corporation.*

Fig. 83. Damp sheets of cellulose and crumbing machine. *American Viscose Corporation.*

sheets, which resemble blotting paper, are washed and bleached, then reduced or shredded to crumbs that are aged in storage at controlled temperatures. After aging, the mass of crumbs (alkali cellulose) is treated with carbon disulfide which changes the material into a soluble (cellulose xanthate).

The final substance, in ball form, is dissolved in a mixer with caustic soda to produce the spinning solution, coludi, which resembles honey or light molasses. The liquid viscose is filtered—and, again, the material is aged, according to the type of rayon intended. Special chemicals are required for dull, semi-dull, or other yarn textures, subduing the high gloss character of formula rayon.

Viscose spinning consists of forcing the solution through a number of fine orifices into an acid bath. The tiny streams of liquid harden into solid filaments which are then bobbin-wound and ready for use.

Another process, pot spinning, twists and shapes the yarn into a cake or cone in a rotating pot. The most recent development is a machine that spins and finishes rayon in a single operation, eliminating handling of skeins and cakes. Viscose rayons are now generally manufactured in one operation—from solution to the twisted thread.

FIBERS

Fig. 84. Liquid cellulose. *American Viscose Corporation.*

Fig. 85. Through spinneret liquid cellulose become solid threads of rayon. *American Viscose Corporation.*

Cuprammonium rayon

This rayon is mostly produced in the United States by the American Bemberg Corporation. It is characterized by extreme fineness of filament. Cuprammonium rayon, in strength and reaction to chemicals, is similar to viscose.

Purified cotton linters are the source of cellulose in this material. The linters are shredded and mixed with copper sulfate and ammonia water in solution. The resulting liquid is filtered and pumped into tanks where it is stored before spinning.

A special process has been developed for yarn making from this synthetic. It is called stretch spinning, which produces thread of great uniformity, strength and fineness. Cuprammonium solution, in stretch spinning, is extruded from the spinneret in filaments collected and forced through a glass water funnel. The water, because of its density, offers resistance to the plastic filaments, decreasing and stretching them as they are drawn forward under tension.

Final hardening of the yarn takes place when groups of filaments leave the funnel and pass through baths of dilute sulfuric acid. After most of the copper in the spinning solution has been removed, the yarn is skeined on reels.

Acetate rayon

This material is manufactured by a process different from viscose and cupra. Acetate rayon has its own reaction to dyestuffs, as well as other individual properties. Direct use of chemical agents, rather than the cellulose regenerating method used in viscose and cupra, creates acetate, or estron. The material is an ester of cellulose, whereas viscose rayon is pure cellulose.

Estron rayon yarn is made from a cellulose-acetate solution drawn through orifices, as in viscose manufacture. In the acetate process, however, the liquid filaments are solidified in hot air chambers where they are twisted and wound on a bobbin, making the finished estron. Acetate thread is somewhat weaker than viscose but has the good qualities of softness and durability. The acetates are much used in apparel fabrics.

Nylon

Research by Du Pont led to the discovery of this synthetic fiber group. Chemically, nylon is an amide. Its amine ingredients are carbon, nitrogen, oxygen and hydrogen, drawn from coal, air and water. Nylon yarn is stretched during spinning. The molecules, or structural elements, are oriented in the direction of the axis—like fibers in worsted or combed cotton—and produces a strong material with some of the characters of natural materials.

Nylon is produced in single filaments or is twisted as rayon and silk are. It also can be cut into staple fibers and spun on the cotton, woolen or worsted systems. Its strength and elasticity made the material an immediate success. Nylon has won the place held by silk in women's hosiery. The thread is colored with acetate dyestuffs, which penetrate the hard yarn.

Resin and plastic thread

These extruded stretch-spun fibers are of very recent origin. The new material (technically, acrylic resin) is sold under the trade name of Orlon. In strength as well as in other characteristics, orlon is related both to rayon and nylon. It is sunfast and suitable for curtains. Its softness and heat-holding qualities give this fiber its wide acceptance.

A special grade of vinyl resin was put on the market in 1930 by the Union Carbide and Carbon Corporation. Several textile fibers have been developed from this resin under the trade name of Vinyon. There are several types, each having different properties. Vinyon is produced by dissolving vinyl resin in acetone. The spinning mixture is filtered and dry spun, like acetate. Unlike most synthetic fibers, vinyon is flat and bandlike. It does not absorb moisture under normal conditions, therefore special agents are used in dyeing vinyon. Chemical filters, garments that must be proof against fire, chemicals and other hazards, and insulation are made from this material.

Most of the plastic fibers are vinylidene chloride, a chemical resin of petroleum and salt. Saran, made from this compound, is produced by Lus-Trus Extruded Plastics, Inc. A similar product, made by Firestone Industrial Products Company, has the trade name Velon.

Saran is manufactured in round filaments and in narrow, rattan-like strips. The resin is non-absorbent, therefore it usually is not dyed. However, pigments are sometimes mixed into the spinning solution. Saran is used for screens, upholstery and handbags.

The various yarns made by Plexon, Inc., under the trade name Plexon, are threads consisting of natural yarns coated with synthetics. The basic thread may be cotton, linen or a rayon, coated with any of twenty-one different resins. The textile properties of Plexon depend on the base and coating used. Since Plexon is strong, flexible and acid resistant, it has numerous good uses.

Glass thread

A hard, brittle substance, chiefly silica, has been made into a versatile glass fiber. Continuous filaments of glass are produced by heating glass shot in electric furnaces. When the material is melted it settles in a v-shaped trough, or furnace, from which it is extruded by spinnerets. Glass filaments are thrown, twisted and wound on bobbins for manufacture.

Yarns

Plain yarns

Yarn consists of two types: plain and novelty. A plain thread is straight, whereas novelties may be uneven and have nubs or other fancy compositions. Much weaving is done with single plain yarn. But, for many purposes, two or more singles are combined in a ply (*Fig. 86*). There are different kinds of yarn twists. In certain fabrics, loosely twisted thread is appropriate; in others, hard twists, such as crêpe. A weaver is also aware of the influence of right- or left-turned yarn on the effect of a cloth.

Singles

A completely untwisted thread that can be directly dissolved into fibers is a single yarn. Woolen yarns are single; silks and rayons are combined singles. These yarns come in heavy and fine qualities.

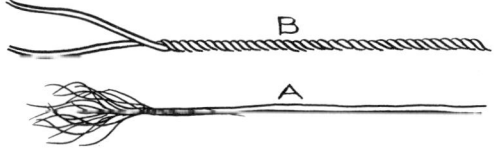

Fig. 86. Yarn constructions. A, single. B, double, or two ply.

Plies

Two or more single yarns twisted together are a ply. The plying is made on a twister frame, almost identical to a ring spinner, except that the yarns are not drawn but twisted together. Described as two-ply, three-ply, and so forth, according to the number of single ends composing the thread, plies are available in infinite combinations.

Twists

It is necessary for many spun yarns to have additional twists. The process of further twisting filament yarns, such as silk, rayon and glass, is called throwing. Twisting operations are sometimes done during spinning but can be done on twister machines according to manufacturing specifications.

Yarns may be given a left-hand "S" or right-hand "Z" twist. Turning is determined by twists per inch or per meter. Warp threads, requiring great strength, are generally given more twist, usually in the "Z" direction. Filling yarns, however, are usually given fewer twists in the "S" direction. The harder the twist, as a rule, the stiffer the yarn. Single yarn, in a ply twist, is customarily turned in the opposite direction from the ply. Double and single twisting in the same direction makes a hard yarn called twist-on-twist.

All fibers, excepting silk, are twisted to the right in single yarns.

Yarn numbering

Yarn sizes are fine, medium, coarse. Since manufacturers have to know the quantity needed, a numbering system based on pound in relation to yarn length has been developed. Each raw material has its specific yarn count, or number. The higher the number, the finer the thread. Number 1 cotton, for example, is based on 840 yards per pound. There is no system for novelty yarns, since the length in these depends on the design of the thread.

Yarn Count
Tables for various yarns

Cotton

No. 1—840 yards per pound.

No. 2—(twice No. 1) 1680 yards per pound.

No. 50—42,000 yards per pound (50 times amount of No. 1).

Number 40/2 cotton has two threads of No. 40 twisted together. The weight of two

No. 40 yarns consequently equals the weight of one No. 20 yarn of the same length. Or, 40/2 is equivalent in weight to 20/1: 20 times 840 yards, 16,800 yards per pound.

Number 60/3 cotton is three threads of 60's, equivalent to the weight of one thread of 20's (No. 20/1).

Wool

No. 1—1600 yards per pound (in woolen yarn, which is not plied).

In worsted yarn, No. 1 is 560 yards per pound. No. 2 worsted is 560 times 2 (1120 yards per pound). Number 40/2 worsted is equal to 20/1 in yards per pound.

Bast fibers

No. 1—300 yards per pound. Bast yarns are usually single, not plied.

Spun silk

No. 1—840 yards per pound.

In spun silk single yarns, the cotton count is used. For the plies, a different count.

Example: a 20/2 spun silk is not 2 ends of 20, but 2 ends of 40, and has the same weight as 20/1.

Silk and rayon

Silks and rayons are not counted in terms of pounds, but deniers, a French measure equal to 528 yards per pound. Silk and rayon dealers provide charts in which weight and length are specified.

Novelties

Traditional weaving was in general representational, done in plain natural yarns. Modern weaving designs are based on simplified geometrical and allover patterns demanding special yarn. Novelty threads are made of combinations of wool, cotton, rayon and other synthetic materials; a few are made entirely of natural fibers. These fancy yarns vary, depending on fashion. The fancier threads are made in coarse numbers, owing to the fact that their structures are elaborate.

Because there is no uniformity in novelty yarn names, it is difficult to identify them. However, we can describe the appearance of the typical ones.

Flake yarn

These popular threads are single and plied. A single flake yarn is composed of fragments of yarn twisted at various distances on a basic thread, or it tapers into a thin strand, and then thickens or flakes again. The flakes often are unevenly spaced the length of the thread. The twist given in spinning has a tendency to affect the thin parts, therefore a great many more turns per inch are found in the thin portions than in the flakes. These yarns can be made from fibers of relatively short length which lend themselves to accurate turning. Most single flake yarns are cotton or staple rayon.

There are several varieties of plied flake yarn. Sometimes, in this type, single flake is combined with ordinary straight thread: a cotton flake with rayon binder, for example. The fancy part also may be of another color from the binder. Unusual combinations consist of two single flakes, or a ply flake, twisted with ordinary thread, the two usually are twisted in opposite directions, thus the ply yarn becomes harder and shorter. This process transforms the soft, long flakes into a bead effect.

Nub yarn

When fine lumps of short fibers are introduced in a wool or cotton yarn, during spinning, nubs are created. This yarn is single, or may be twisted with regular threads. Wool

FIBERS

is the most adaptable material for this novelty. The nubs, which are often a different color from the ground color of the thread, are composed of fibers crossed in all directions and introduced during carding. Unlike flake yarns, the added particles are unevenly spaced and simply laid and turned on the basic thread. Nub yarn is much used in weaving fancy woolen fabrics.

Knop yarn

Knop and nub yarns are confused because of the similarity of their names. However, a knop yarn has really hard knots, or particles of hard, twisted thread, quite unlike the soft, short bits in nub yarn. When two or more ground threads are twisted in the construction of knop yarn, one thread is let off slowly and intermittently, the other rapidly and continuously. The faster turning thread forms bunches called knops.

The hard knop occurs in different shapes and the yarn is characterized by extreme contrast between knops and basic thread. The knops slide readily along the yarn, therefore a thread—often of contrasting

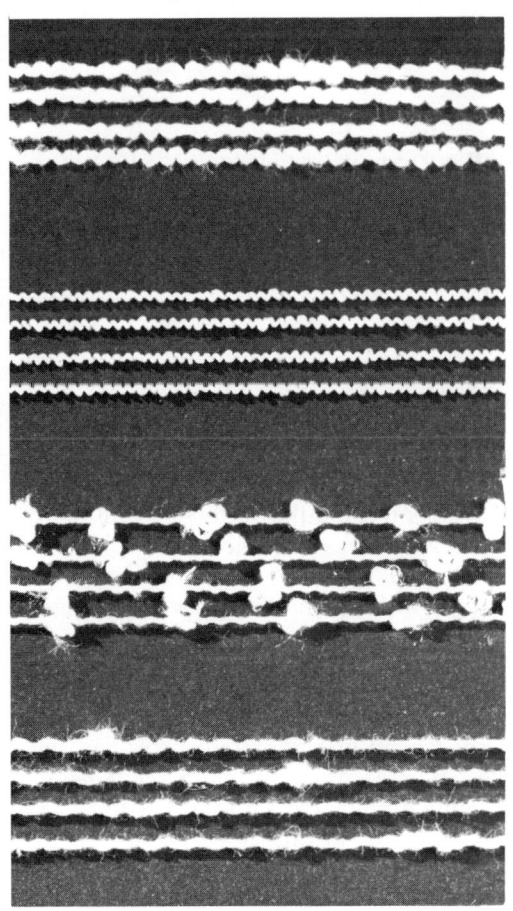 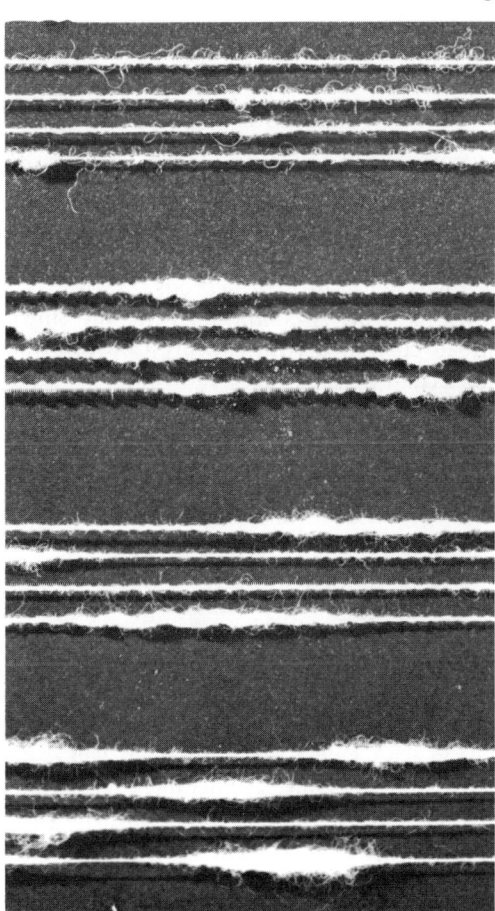

Fig. 87. Novelty yarns. From top to bottom: (left) ratine, spiral, loop yarn, knop yarn, (right) nub yarn, two examples of flake ply yarn, single flake.

color and fiber—is twisted around the knop to prevent sliding. This design is called knotted twist. It is the most usual knop type.

Loop yarn

Wool and rayon loop, or curly, yarn is another one of the popular novelties. Its manufacture is similar to that of the knop and nub yarns. The binder ends are twisted in the usual manner, but a third end is let off in jerks, during twisting, to form kinked and curled loops at regular intervals.

Spiral and ratine

Spiral yarn consists of two single ends twisted—one delivered faster than the other and wound around the more slowly rotating thread. Sometimes a hard-twist single end and one softer single are turned together, or a thick and thin are combined. Spiral yarns of many colors and variations are produced by these, the principal methods.

Ratine yarn is composed of a fine single thread combined with two-ply twisted yarn, the second twist opposite the first. The twisting opens the spiral yarn in a softly linked chain. Ratines are cotton, spun rayon and worsted. The spiral yarns usually are cotton or rayon.

Chenille and other novelties

Chenille yarn is not twisted. It is a thread that has been cut from woven goods in yarn-like strips. In weaving the material from which chenille is made, four to eight warp ends are spaced an equal distance apart, and woven with heavy filling in plain weave or leno. After weaving, a machine cuts the filling between the woven strips, thus producing a thread highly suitable for handweavers' designs.

Novelties can be varied, two kinds combined. Contrast of color and raw material also plays a distinct part in the creation of effect yarns. Light and dark threads may be used in twists of ratine and flake, or a cotton base used with rayon binders. Gold and silver thread, split bamboo, ribbon, raffia, and many other materials are marketed for weavers to experiment with.

Dyeing

There are various methods of applying dyes to weavers' raw materials. Coloring raw fiber is called stock dyeing. Yarns also are dyed after spinning, according to the proposed design. The kind of dye used depends largely on effect desired, as well as cost.

Stock

Wool, cotton, rayon staple, and waste silk may be colored in the raw stock. This is done in a rotation cylinder in which the fibers circulate in a dye bath. In another type, the water circulates and the fibers remain stationary. In the latter, a cylinder is packed with the fiber stock and immersed in a dye tank. The revolving cylinder forces the liquid through the stock.

Skein

In this method the skeins, or yarn hanks, are hung on rods in a machine containing the dye liquid. The rods are revolved and submerged with the yarns in heated dye.

Cop

Yarns from the spinning frame are sometimes wound on perforated spools and spindles and placed in a dye bath, the liquid circulating through the yarns. This type of dyeing also is done with warp threads on perforated beams.

These are the chief dyeing methods, but there are many others.

Part III. Weaves

MOST OF the textiles we use in our daily life are made on a loom. Some raw materials, however, may be transformed into cloth by other methods than weaving. For example, knitted and net fabrics are formed by hand or machine needles from a continuous thread in interlocking loops. Weaving, is, simply, the interlacing of two yarn groups at right angles.

The lengthwise groups in weaving are strung side by side and wound firmly around a beam in back of the loom (*Fig.* 88). These vertical threads stretch toward the weaver, who sits at the front of the loom where the yarns are fastened to the front beam. The taut threads are the warp, or foundation, for weaving. Each thread in a warp is called an end, or warp end. The selvages of the fabric are the last warp threads on either side of the group.

The cross-yarn system, or weft (filling), consists of consecutive horizontal threads, interlaced at right angles with the warp. The weft yarn is wound on a spool fitted in a shuttle, and served through the warp.

The warp ends are lifted in groups (*Fig.* 89). Some of the ends are raised while others are kept down, creating a division, or space, called shed. The weft in the shuttle passes through this opening between the warp yarns, making a pick, or single weft, across the loom. Successive shifting of lifted warp ends for each pick creates the interlacing known as weave.

The closest warp-and-weft weaving resembles mending. It is called plain weave—in which a single warp thread passes over one pick and under the next throughout the cloth. The following warp end runs under that pick and over the next.

A unit, in plain weave, is composed of two warp ends and two wefts. For one pick,

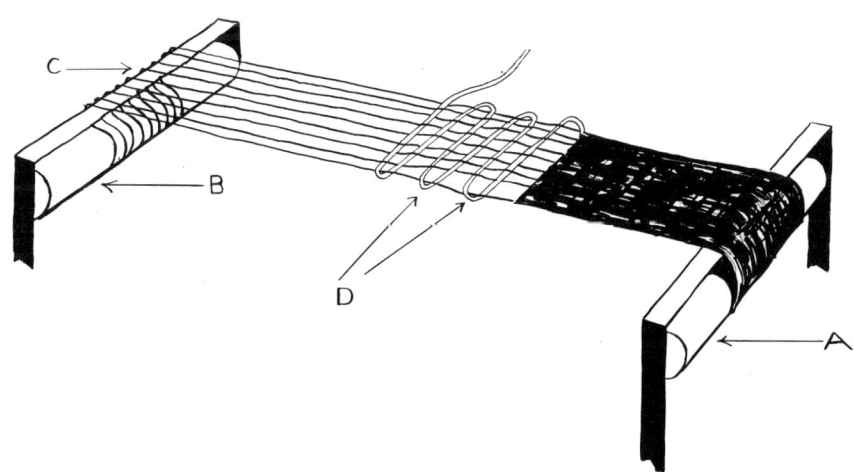

Fig. 88. Warp threads (C) interlace with weft (D). (A) cloth beam, (B) warp beam.

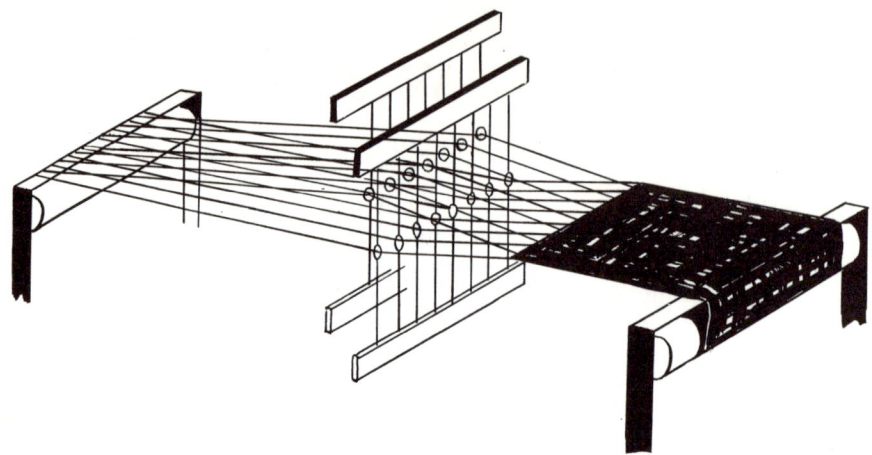

Fig. 89. Warp-lifting shafts creating shed.

odd-numbered ends are raised and for the following weft even-numbered threads come up, passing over the weft while the odd group is down and hidden (*Fig. 90*).

There are unlimited varieties of interlacing besides plain weave. Weaves begin with basic constructions, but can have as many as twenty-five different changes within a unit, depending on the design. A weave is completed when every weft is interlaced with another group of warp ends. A unit is usually repeated throughout a fabric. Interlacing determines the structure and appearance of a textile. Each foundation weave has its distinctive character and surface of ribbed, smooth, or other effect.

Drafting Symbols of Weaves

Weaves usually are drawn and read on graph paper, a system used by designers everywhere. The symbols of interlacing order are represented on paper to simplify procedure, but woven fabric will never have the appearance of our paper conception.

A weave, or interlacing, made with fine thread looks the same on paper as one of heavy thread, but in the actual weaving two different weights of fabric result. The design on paper, for all weights of thread, will always have the same dimension and appearance. Drafting generously helps the weaver

Fig. 90. Plain weave interlacing, enlarged.

visualize. The paper makes him know the interlacings, giving impressions that become his repertoire of techniques.

Ordinary graph paper used for design contains eight or ten rows of checked squares. Each vertical row of small squares represents a lengthwise thread or warp end as it will appear on the loom. The horizontal checks indicate weft, or filling. The vertical checks symbolize warp ends placed side by side, without space between them.

Graph paper of ten-by-ten checks per heavily ruled block is used in this book, as per sample (*Fig.* 91). The heavy ruling of each block helps the eye count checks.

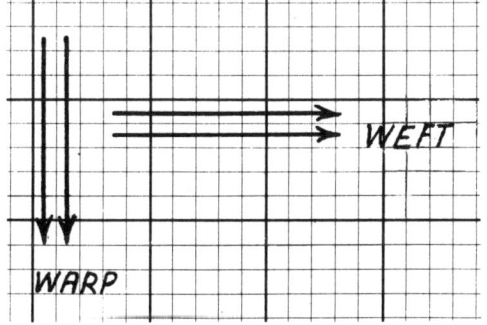

Fig. 91. Draft paper: vertical direction warp, horizontal weft.

In time, we learn weaves by heart and depend less on paper, but here we are concerned with fundamentals.

A weaver's complete draft, or layout on paper, will represent three ideas:

the weave, or pattern of interlacing;
the plan for threading the warp through heddle eyes;
tie-up, or shaft-and-treadle connection.

Drafting

Interlacings, or weaves, are indicated by marking or filling in some checks while others are left blank. When a square is marked, the weaver knows that the warp end of that vertical row of squares is to be lifted for that particular weft. The weft, represented by the horizontal checks, is underneath this warp end. The warp end is on the surface and raised over the weft.

When a square is left blank, it indicates that the warp end represented by that vertical row is lowered at that point, and also that the weft represented by the horizontal row of squares is on top of the warp. Marked, or filled-in, squares always mean warp up, weft covered (*Fig.* 92).

The illustration is a drafted plain weave.

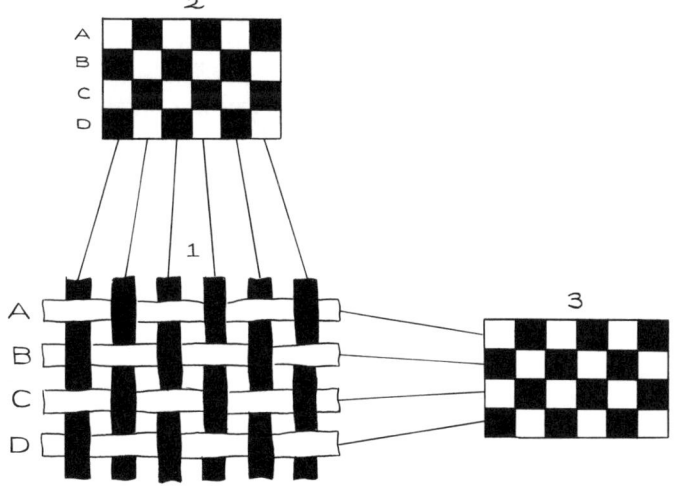

Fig. 92. (1) Plain weave structure, ABCD representing weft (3). Black threads relate to warp draft (2).

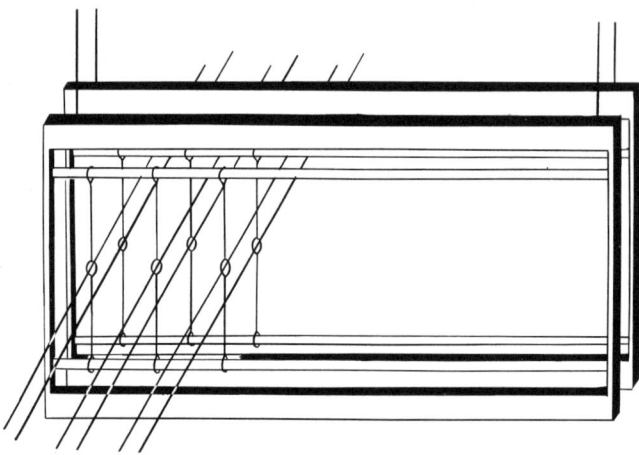

Fig. 93. Two shafts threaded straight draw.

The first horizontal row of squares is alternately filled in. The second row alternates with the first. The design shows that in the first row even-numbered warp ends are to be raised, while for the second row, the odd-numbered threads will be raised.

The heddles, which are strung on the shafts, or frames at the center of the loom, are the device for lifting warp ends. Entering yarns through the heddle eyes is of special importance, since a weave depends on the threading order or the drawing-in of the warp. Of standard threading drafts the most useful is straight draw. On a loom with two shafts, half the warp yarns are put through heddle eyes on one shaft, the other half through the eyes on the second shaft.

The first warp end is usually drawn through the first heddle eye on the shaft nearest the weaver. The second yarn goes through the first eye on the second shaft. This is repeated throughout the threading of the entire warp (*Fig.* 93). Thus, when shaft one is lifted, all the odd-numbered threads rise in one movement.

Straight draw is done with any number of shafts, sometimes as many as eight. Warp yarns threaded on only two shafts, straight draw, produce a limited weave variety, such as plain weave, with alternating warp yarns either up or down.

Threading-draws are symbolized on draft paper (*Fig.* 94). Since the shafts hang horizontally in the loom, the horizontal rows of checks represent shafts. If a weave requires two shafts, two rows of checks are all that are needed. But for more elaborate weaves, with four shafts, as shown, the weaver uses

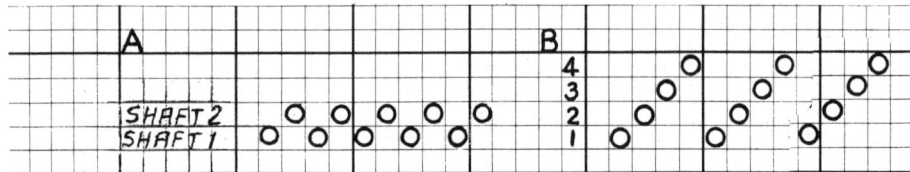

Fig. 94. (A) Straight warp-threading draft for two shafts, (B) same for four shafts.

four rows of checks for his threading plan. His drafting symbol for heddle eyes will be a loop, or circle, marked in the square, representing an opening through which a warp thread is to be drawn.

Warp ends that need to be raised for a weft are usually all on one shaft. But, for the following, or alternate weft, another group will be lifted, requiring its proper shaft. Every warp thread that represents a new interlacing is drawn through the heddle eyes on the shaft proper to it. In plain weave, on two shafts, the odd-numbered threads rise over a weft in a single movement; therefore all these threads come through heddle eyes on the same shaft. The change takes place in lifting the warp for the weft following. These warp threads, the even-numbered, are threaded through the eyes in the second heddle frame.

The illustration (*Fig.* 95) is a draft for plain weave. The horizontal rows of checks

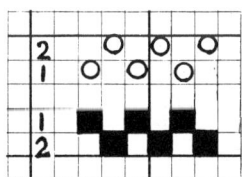

Fig. 95. Plain weave draft for two shafts, circles indicate warp-threading order.

are used. The first row has six alternating squares filled in. The following row is marked in reverse, starting with a blank. The threading order, or next step, is usually indicated above the weave. Two horizontal rows of checks are customarily omitted, the third row above the weave representing the first shaft. A circle is marked in the first square in the vertical or warp row where the draft begins. That is to say, the first filled-in square in the draft is the first thread in the warp.

Since the second warp end on the first weft is down, a new shaft is needed. A circle is made in the row above the first shaft indication. This symbol represents the second warp thread, however, and is in the vertical row, above the first blank square in the first plain weave row. In brief, the illustration shows that the first warp end goes through the first heddle eye on the first shaft, the second thread through the first eye on the second shaft. The rotation is repeated until all yarns are threaded.

To find the threading order, a weave draft is read from top to bottom, row after row. Each warp end that interlaces or binds differently on the same weft requires another shaft. In order to know the threading draft for a particular weave, this top-to-bottom reading method is the same in simple and complicated weaving. The order of drawing-in is varied, according to the variety of warp lifting in a unit. At present, the emphasis is on paper representation of threading drafts in general.

A two-shaft loom always has two treadles. The shaft that hangs in front is connected with one treadle, and the shaft behind with the other. If all odd threads on the first shaft happen to be up for the first weft, the treadle connecting with the even number shaft is pushed down. The two treadles are simply alternated, back and forth, opening and closing the shed, constructing a plain weave.

The tie-up of shaft and treadle is put on graph paper. We use an x-symbol to designate this tie-up, or connection. If the first weft requires shaft up, an x-mark is made at the end of the same horizontal row as the

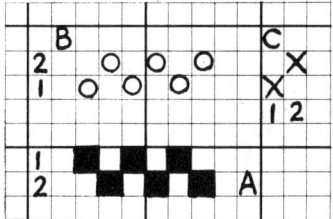

Fig. 96. (1) Warp lifting indication for tie-up in plain weave interlacing (A). Warp-threading order (B).

threading circles. The following tie-up mark is indicated on the next vertical row, at right, in line with the circles of the second shaft (*Fig. 96*).

In beginning, it is best to number all weft rows. The shafts representing warp threads should also be numbered. Each vertical row of x-marks represents a treadle corresponding with its horizontal weft row.

The first thing in weaving, as well as reading the graph, is knowing which shaft to raise—which treadle to operate—in order to admit the weft to its right shed. This basic operation is always mechanical and depends on the loom—the number of shaft-and-treadle connections available and used by the weaver for his design. Accordingly, where multi-shaft looms are used, the weaver's graph will be the same as, but more complex than, the examples above.

Entering or threading draws

Although straight threading is basic and practical, many patterns dictate their own threading. Every yarn in the warp that interlaces in a different way with the filling must be drawn through its own harness in the loom. On the other hand, every warp yarn that interlaces alike with the weft is threaded on the same shaft as the previous end (*Figs. 97, 98*).

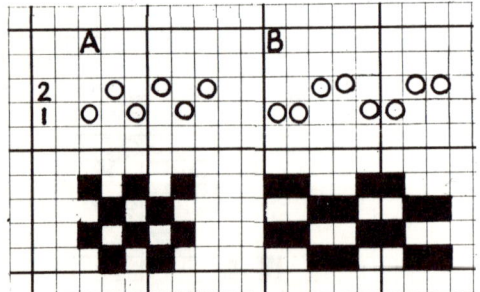

Fig. 97. (A) Threading order and draft of odd-numbered warp yarns on shaft 1, and even-numbered on shaft 2. (B) Side-by-side indication of two threads in the same order as A.

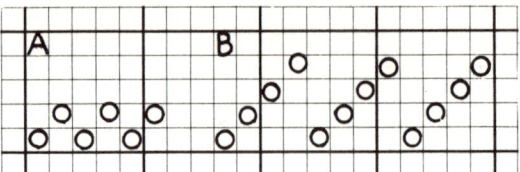

Fig. 98. (A) Straight threading draft on two shafts, (B) on four shafts.

Terms for threading variations are *skip, point, broken, section,* and *combination.*

Skip draw (*Fig. 99*) requires at least four shafts. The threading is scattered. In plain weave with this draw, shafts 1 and 2 alternate with 3 and 4.

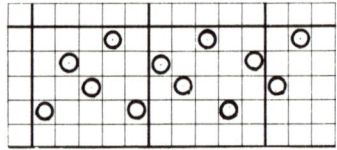

Fig. 99. Skip threading draft on four shafts.

Point draw (*Fig. 100*), resulting from straight draw, runs first in one direction (front to back) and then in the other (back to front). The shaft at each point of reversal receives only one thread, the other shafts carrying two ends each for the resulting double line. The unit of ends in one of the illustrated examples is six. In the other, the threading order is repeated every fourteen warp threads. The yarn at either reversal or change in direction is the point thread. To vary the length of the lines in either direction, two or more points may be brought into one draft. If irregular intervals are intended, the point yarns may be threaded on different shafts and arranged for an equal number of heddles on each harness.

Point draw is usually required in herringbone patterns. The size of a herringbone depends on the number of yarns per inch—the quality, or yarn set. For example, if the pattern should be two inches zigzag, twenty

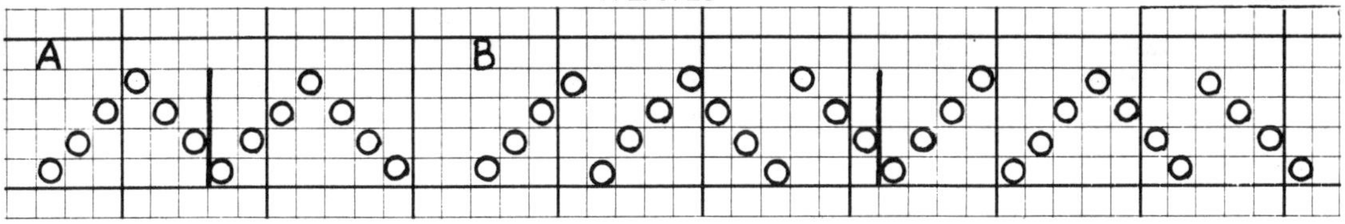

WEAVES

Fig. 100. Point threading draft with units of 6 and 14 threads (A and B, respectively).

ends per inch is the quality. Twenty warp threads for one direction are entered from front to back, with the reverse threaded back to front for another twenty ends.

Broken draw (*Fig.* 101): one group of threads drawn straight in one direction, with alternate group reversed. When the direction is reversed the first end of the new series is started higher—or lower—than the last thread of the preceding. In a herringbone, woven from the illustrated draft, the pattern will show a distinct break at the point of reversal. Where the twill reverses or slants in opposition, the last end of one stripe interlaces in contrast to the first end in the next twill line. Broken is preferred to point draw because it results in better interlacing.

Section or group draw (*Figs.* 102, 103) for vertical stripes, checks, and other fancy effects in which two weaves are employed:

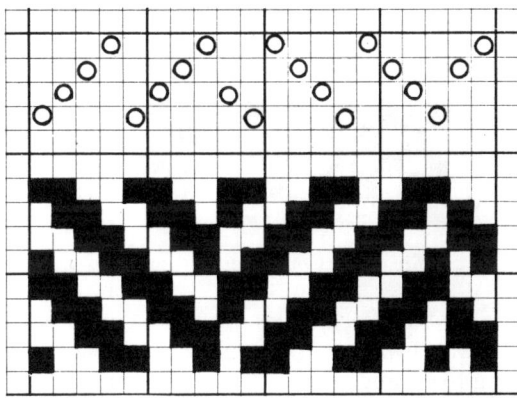

Fig. 101. Broken, or uneven, threading with draft of weave (herringbone).

ends for each weave are threaded on their own shafts. The section draw illustrated shows eight ends entered straight on four shafts. Another set of four frames is used for the following group of yarns. The first section interlaces in weft twill, while the second group (shafts 5, 6, 7, 8) is warp twill on the same pick.

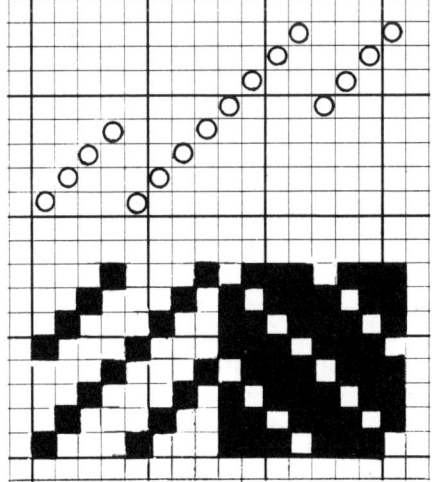

Fig. 102. Section threading on 8 shafts and weave design.

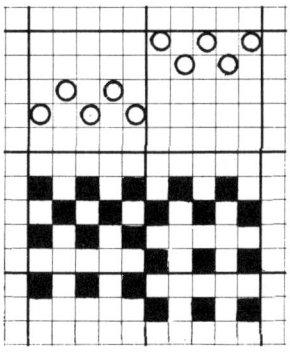

Fig. 103. Section threading on 4 shafts and design.

Combination draw: This is several drawing orders in one draft. The example (*Fig. 104*) is simple, but in this draw, of course, variety is unlimited.

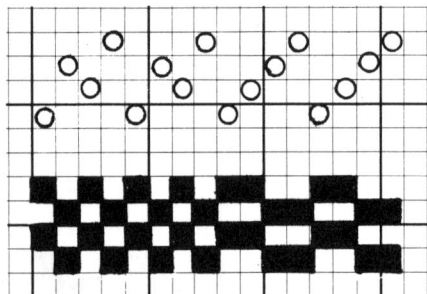

Fig. 104. Combination threading.

All these techniques are bases for threading. Drawing-in drafts are changed according to desired weaves. Usually we choose the simplest style, being limited by the number of harnesses on the loom. Some weaves, however, can be arranged to fit small as well as large numbers of shafts.

Foundation Weaves

There are three fundamental constructions: plain, twill, and satin. Derivative weaves are created from these basic types. Intricate patterns in weaving consist of combining a standard construction, such as twill, with either plain or satin weave. In most fabrics we can easily recognize yarn groups interlacing in one or more of the basic types.

While having a character of its own, each weave may be used in any number of ways and qualities of fabric. Plain weave is equally effective in heavy and fine cloth. A twill effect, intended for upholstery, may also be used for suitings.

In the study of foundation weaves and how to make them, weaving drafts of units are illustrated. The unit is indicated with shaded checks, the repeats filled-in with black.

Plain weave

This is the basic construction—the closest interlacing of warp and filling. All of the threads appear equal on the surface of both sides of the material. Plain weave (*Fig. 105*) is a most familiar construction. We encounter it daily. Plain-woven cloth usually has a smooth effect and less elasticity than fabrics of complex interlacing. Effective cloth, however, is created in plain weave by choice of yarn and color.

Fig. 105. Plain weave.

A plain-weave unit consists of two warp and two filling threads. At one pick, each alternate warp end is raised above the filling; the other warp ends are hidden under the weft. This order is reversed in the next pick. In the first, the odd-numbered ends were raised, but now, in the following weft, the even-numbered ends are up, and cover

WEAVES

the filling. The illustration (*Fig.* 106) is the draft for plain weave. The design unit is shaded and the repeats, or raised warp ends, are indicated in black. The white checks always represent weft.

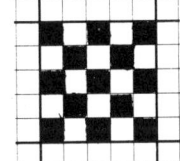

Fig. 106. Draft of plain weave.

Twill weaves

Twill weave (*Fig.* 107) has a more distinct surface structure than plain weave. In twill, single warp ends, as well as the picks, cover more than one thread. To make this interlacing we need at least three ends and three picks to form the unit, which is repeated. Warp ends, as well as filling, cover two threads and interlace with the third. Rotation of basic three-end twill units is always consecutive. The rotation changes with each succeeding pick, one warp thread to the right, as in the illustration.

The illustrated twill (*Fig.* 108) is formed by one warp thread raised in one place, the ends on either side being lowered. The first warp yarn covers the first filling, the second end passes over the second weft, and the third on top of the third pick—the last before the repeat. Thus the characteristic diagonally ribbed lines of twill are formed.

The weave is classified in two groups: uneven and balanced twill. Uneven twills are those in which the warp is on the surface more often than the weft. A warp-predominated surface is called warp twill; and with weft predominating, weft twill. In balanced twills, both warp and weft are in equal surface distribution, forming a reversible fabric.

Fig. 107. Twill weave.

The illustration (*Fig.* 108, A and B) shows uneven twills, repeated after each unit of three ends and three picks. These weaves require at least three shafts, straight-draw threaded.

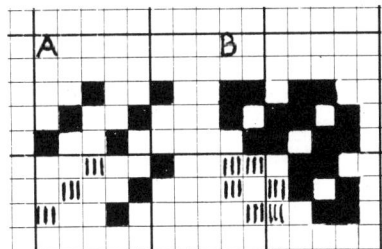

Fig. 108. Draft of (A) weft, and (B) 3-end twills. Shaded checks show the unit; the black are its repeat.

Illustration 109 represents uneven twills of four-warp and four-weft units. These require four shafts, straight-draw threaded. Eight shafts also could be used, multiplying by two the unit of four-end repeat.

A unit of four ends and four picks will form a balanced twill, as illustrated (*Fig.* 110), with half warp up, half down, evenly distributed, as is the case in all reversible twills.

The diagonal formed in the twill may be to right or left, and these weaves are right- or left-hand twill. Fabrics with twill are more pliable than plain weave, thus most of our woolen coat materials are variations of twill. In this weave, there is no alternate interlacing as in plain weave. There are few intersections of warp and weft, thus allowing scope for making various qualities of cloth. A twill fabric may be thick, heavy, loose or flexible, as desired.

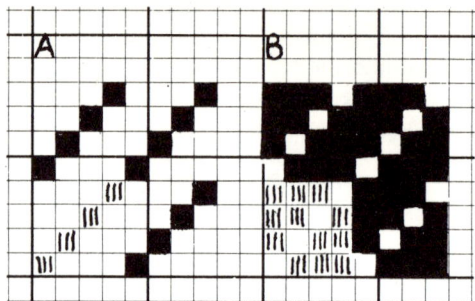

Fig. 109. (A) weft, and (B) warp twills (uneven).

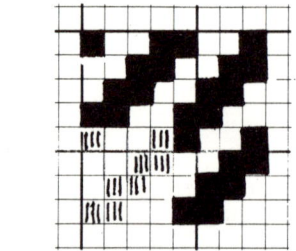

Fig. 110. Even-sided, or reversible, 4-end twill.

Satin weave

In satin weave (*Fig.* 111) the diagonal lines of twills are absent. The interlacing points of warp and weft are not consecutive but widely scattered. The arrangement of warp and stitchers, intersections of warp and weft, in satin weave creates an entirely smooth surface. The farther apart the stitchers, or binding points, the more indistinct these weave intersections will be, creating a satin smoothness.

A basic satin weave requires at least a five-end unit, made on five shafts, straight draw. Any number of shafts, however, may be employed.

Satin construction is as follows: In simple weft twills, the distance from the warp-on-top-of-filling mark to the warp indication for the following pick is one at a time, to right or left. In this cloth the intersections, or crossings, are made by adjacent warp ends. There is no consecutive order in satins.

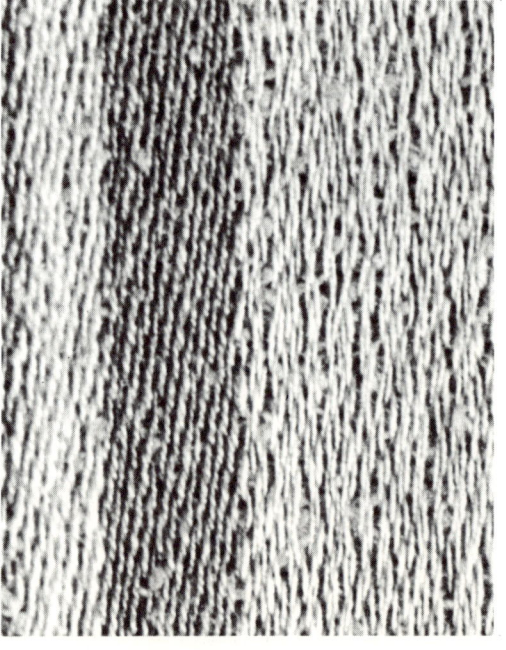

Fig. 111. Warp satin.

We follow a formula called counter. To find the counter, divide the number of warp threads in a pattern in two strictly unequal parts. Either of these unequal units of warp threads may be used as a counter, but the smaller unit usually is preferred. Two or three is the counter in five-end satin, whereas in an eight-end unit three or five may be taken.

The illustration (*Fig.* 112) is a five-end satin made with counter two. We begin with the filled-in square, raised warp end, on the first pick, progressing two warp threads to the right on each following weft. Thus the ends for this satin are stitched in the following order: first warp thread is stitched (or on top) of first pick. For the following or second weft, the third end is raised. On the third pick, the fifth warp end is up, and the fourth weft is interlaced with the second end. For the last, or fifth, pick, the fourth end covers the filling. Counting, or marking, the stitchers is done in one direction throughout the unit, either to right or left.

There are two kinds of satin weave—warp and weft—depending on which element dominates the weave. In warp satin, warp dominates the surface of the fabric; in weft satin, weft is predominant. Illustrated (*Fig.* 113) is a warp satin with counter two for weft crossing. A weft satin made on eight shafts is also illustrated (*Fig.* 114). All these satin weaves require straight draw.

A satin weave is used for fine fabrics in which close sets of warp ends are employed. These fabrics, no longer popular in handweaving, demand at least forty or fifty ends per inch, the interlacing points of warp and weft being much farther apart than in plain or twill weave. However, the long stitches from one binding point to the next expose to advantage the shiny silk threads characteristic in damasks. The figure or ornament in damask is formed by a weft satin on warp-effect background. The combination creates contrasting light reflections.

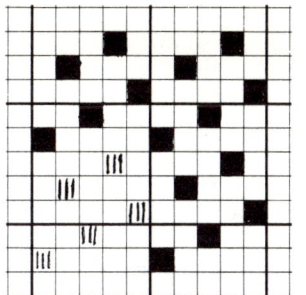

Fig. 112. Draft of 5-end weft satin.

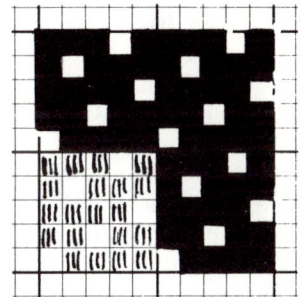

Fig. 113. Five-end warp satin.

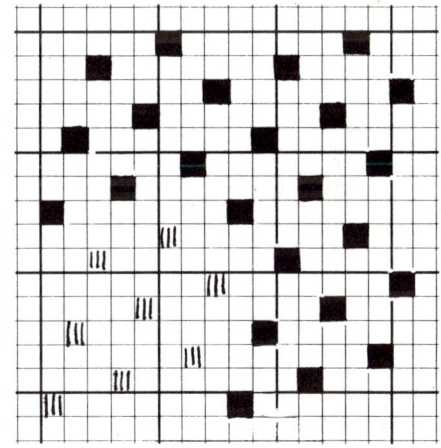

Fig. 114. Eight-end weft satin.

Satin construction is used in all branches of weaving; in wools to produce doeskins, and in cotton for sateens. A damask linen tablecloth is made with contrasting warp- and-weft satin weaves. Stripe effects, modern or antique, also include the warp or weft satin effects.

Derivative Weaves

The above descriptions show how the three elementary weaves are constructed, their drawing-in order through heddle eyes on shafts, as well as some of their special characteristics. Plain weave, twill and satin may be transformed into other patterns. These variations on basic constructions are called derivative weaves, which have their proper names and techniques.

Basic plain weave may be rearranged. In its fundamental construction, a single warp end goes over one pick and under the next, the adjacent end interlacing alternately. This two-end unit, repeated throughout the remaining ends, can be enlarged into a four-end pattern by repeating each single end in the plain weave order. The first and second threads together may go over a pick and be hidden under the following weft. Warp ends three and four will then move in the opposite order—plain-weave style—under one pick and over the next (*Fig.* 115).

of a pick while another is below the same pick, these ends must be on separate shafts.

Illustrated (*Fig.* 116) are two warp ends to be drawn on different shafts. Their variation in warp and weft interlacing is arrow-marked in the graph. The following illustrations (*Figs.* 117, 118) also show orders of intersection woven on two shafts.

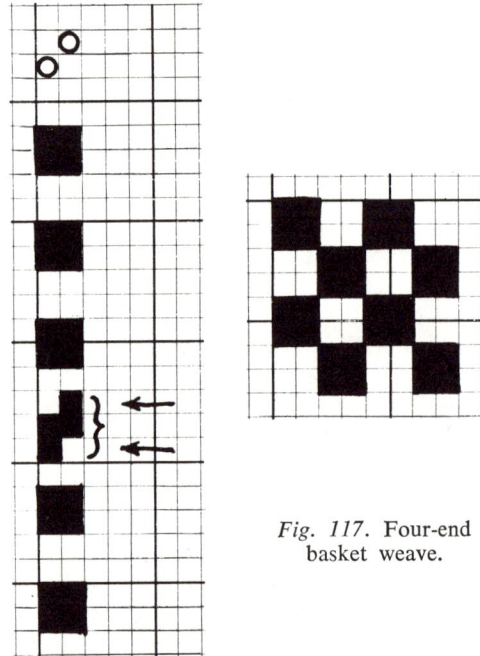

Fig. 117. Four-end basket weave.

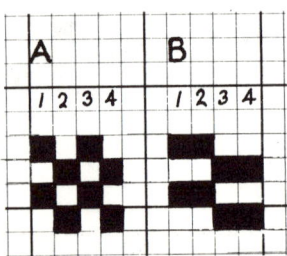

Fig. 115. (A) plain weave, (B) plain weave enlarged.

Elaboration of elementary weaves will often require changes in threading order. Warp ends will be drawn on the same shaft that interlaces the filling, in one order, from start to finish of the pattern. If, at one place in the draft, or unit, a warp thread is on top

Fig. 116. Two warp ends drawn on different shafts. Arrows indicate point of change in interlacing.

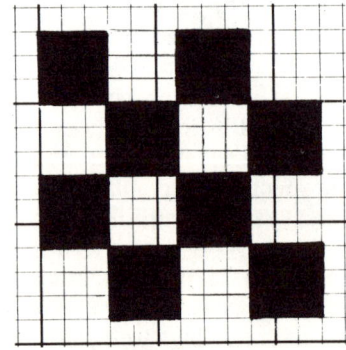

Fig. 118. Six-end basket weave.

WEAVES

A four-end weft twill (*Fig.* 119) having four different orders of intersection requires four shafts, straight draw. Threading indications may be marked above or below a weave. All the entering draws, in these examples, are made above the weave draft.

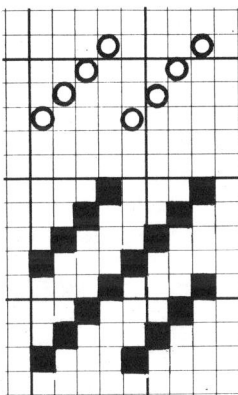

Fig. 119. Threading order and design for 4-end weft twill.

Basket weave

This is enlarged plain weave. Two or more adjacent warp and filling threads are raised and lowered like a single thread. Basket weaves are checkerboard effects, on account of the massing of threads, and may be small or large squares, mixed to create surface variation.

Simple basket weave is a repeat of four warp ends and four wefts (*Fig.* 120, A and B). The pattern is made with either two or four shafts. Thread ends one and two on the first shaft, each through separate heddles, are used in making the first example. Warp ends three and four will be on the following or second shaft. This order is repeated throughout a warp. The illustration shows that the weft in this example alternates, as in plain weave, but only double picks are used.

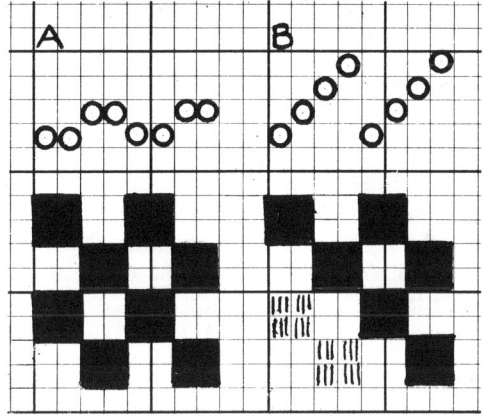

Fig. 120. (A) Basket weave on 2, and (B) on 4 shafts.

The four-end basket weave, woven on four shafts, requires straight draw. The first double filling is created by raising shafts one and two together and, in the following pick, shafts three and four, as illustrated. The filling used in these examples consists of two threads, double-wound on the spool in the shuttle. Back-and-forth insertion of these threads, done only once, will achieve basket repeat in the weft. The illustration (*Fig.* 121) represents a six-end basket weave.

These are examples of equal squares, in which two or more warp ends are similarly

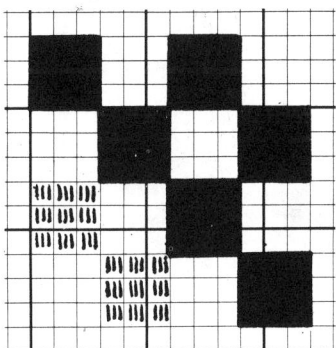

Fig. 121. Shaded units of 6-end basket weave and their repeats.

interlaced. In the illustration, however (*Fig. 122*), a design for mixing large and small squares is introduced. Illustrations (*Figs. 123, 124*) show use of single ends alternating with regular basket weave.

Both styles—equal squares, as well as irregular basket weave—are used in all kinds of fabrics. Density and quality of yarn govern the effect of these designs. Basket weave is not a close interlacing. The filling threads slide and shift more easily than in other intersected constructions.

Rib weave

Cross and lengthwise ribs are also derived from plain weave. Simple forms of cross rib are very much like plain weave. The distinction is in the filling order. Use for each pick, in simple cross rib, a fine doubled thread, or a heavy weft, to contrast with warp threads. Illustrated (*Fig.* 125) is a cross rib which can be made on either two or four shafts. It can be varied with alternating fine and coarse weft (*Fig.* 126). Prepare the doubled yarn for the filling, as in basket weave, so that each pick of several threads is woven as one thread. Other cross ribs may be made with three, four or more picks in one shed, depending on rib thickness desired.

Lengthwise ribs are many yarns woven as

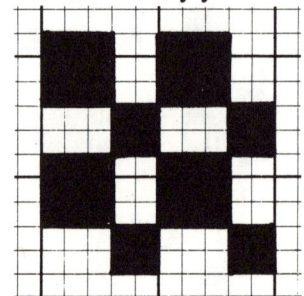

Fig. 122. Basket weave, irregular.

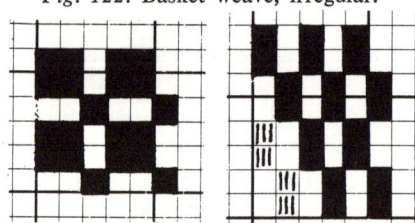

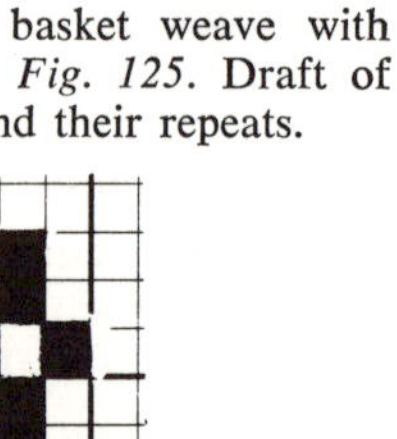

Fig. 123. Irregular basket weave with single warp threads. *Fig. 125.* Draft of cross rib units and their repeats.

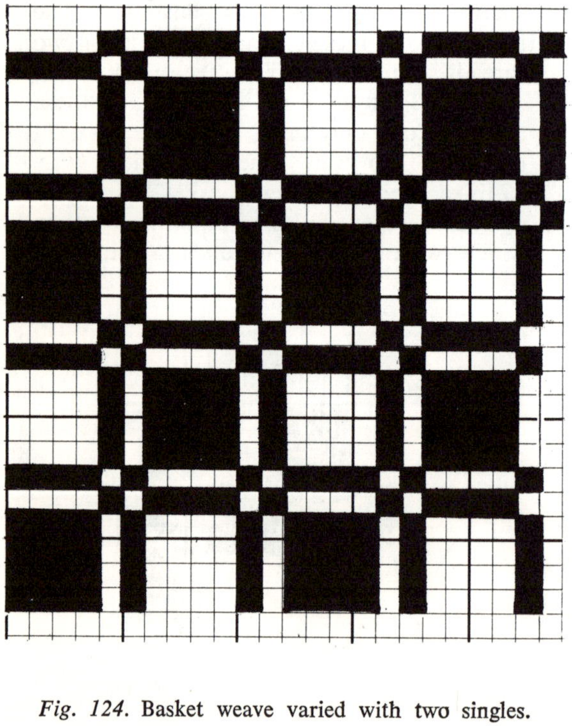

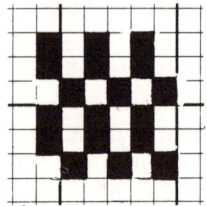

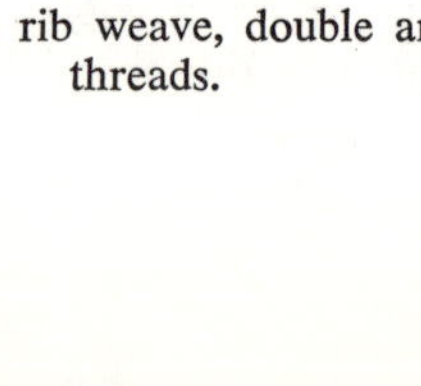

Fig. 126. Cross rib weave, double and single threads.

Fig. 124. Basket weave varied with two singles.

WEAVES

one thread. Basic long rib is enlarged plain weave in which a group of warp threads are raised and lowered together, as illustrated (*Fig.* 127) using either two or four shafts, or in the following illustration, using four shafts straight draw, each heddle threaded with four single yarns to be interlaced as in plain weave, odd and even alternating.

In regular long rib (*Fig.* 127) the warp is almost covered by the filling construction —a design technique used in sturdy or stiff materials. This is the weave employed in tapestries and rugs.

These examples of cross-and-lengthwise rib are only an introduction. They may be elaborated as combination rib (*Fig.* 128) in which the pattern space is divided in four equal parts. Sections are filled in with cross rib and the draft is completed by reserving the remaining squares for rib of lengthwise construction. To vary this, make one rib the

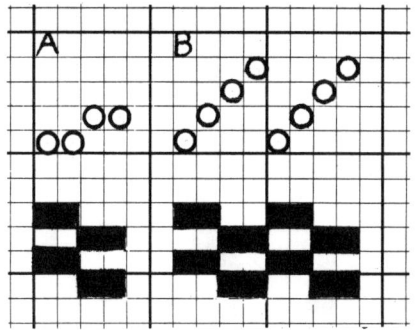

Fig. 127. Lengthwise rib. (A) on 2 shafts, (B) on 4.

motif and use contrasting structure as background.

Twill Variation

Fundamental twills may be arranged in new, or created, patterns. We can reverse the direction of the twill line at intervals, in both

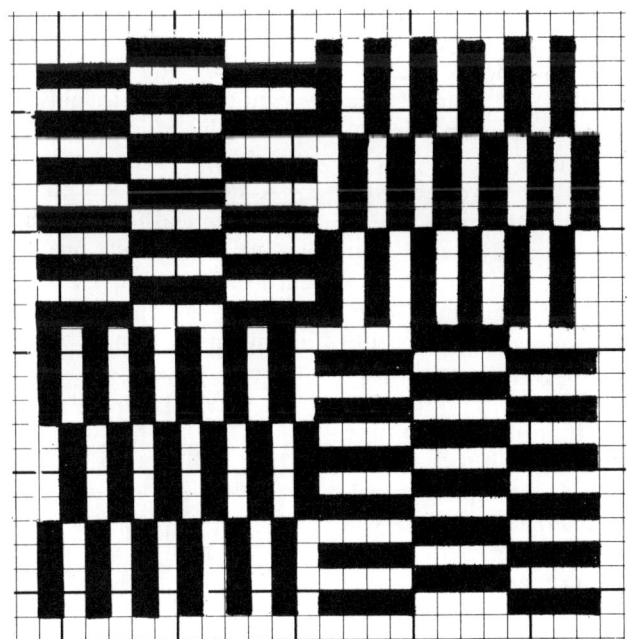

Fig. 128. Cross and lengthwise ribs combined.

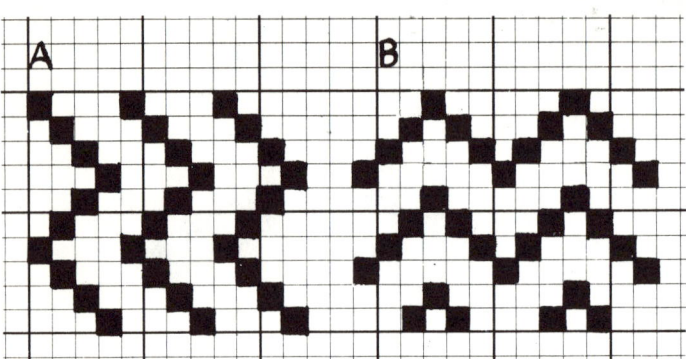

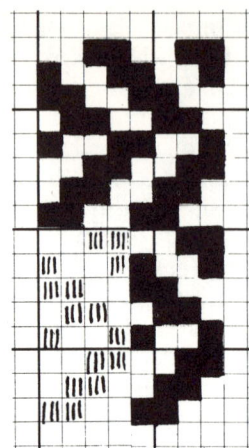

Fig. 129. (A) weft direction, (B) warp, in a reversed twill.

Fig. 130. Cross rib, evensided twill.

warp and weft direction (*Fig.* 129). When we use a left-to-right twill for four picks and change, slanting it to the left for another four, a zigzag motif is determined. We can use this system for all twills, balanced or unbalanced. The zigzag variations create stripes, and if reversing is done in the weft, the stripe is horizontal. In order to make a lengthwise stripe in the direction of the warp, reverse the twill, making on this account a special entering draw.

Illustrated (*Fig.* 130) is a reversed twill, weftwise, filling way. The pattern is called twill cross rib. Begin the weave with four picks of regular balanced twill and follow with four picks woven in reverse. On account of the fourth and fifth pick, a contrast stripe is created. The point of reversal or change of direction consists of contrary weft interlacings. Ends one and four are raised in the fourth weft, the contrasting fifth pick requiring warp threads two and three up, or raised, to make the contrary interlacing. Thus, twill cross rib may be started anywhere within the twill unit by making four picks in rotation and raising the lowered, or hidden, warp threads at the point of reversal, creating a reversed unit.

The illustration (*Fig.* 131) is also an example of reversed or transposed twill, less pronounced than striped weave and based on regular four end weft twill. Raise warp end one for the first pick, then second warp end for second pick, but for reversing, interrupt the twill line and lift warp end four. Complete the unit with third warp end raised, that is, on top of the weft. Both weft-reversed twills are straight draw on four shafts.

The illustration (*Fig.* 132) is a reversed or broken design based on four-end warp twill. For the first weft raise warp threads two, three and four together. For the following weft raise ends one, two and four. The third pick will require warp yarns one, three and four on top of the weft. In the last filling, warp ends one, two and three are lifted.

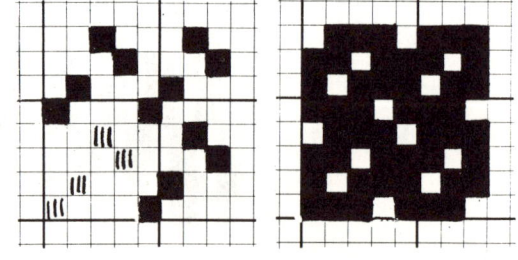

Fig. 131. (*Left*) Transposed twill. Fig. 132. (*Right*) Warp twill reversed.

WEAVES

In herringbone the twill line is broken, reversed, in the warp. The illustration (*Fig.* 133) shows this popular weave, used in apparel fabrics. Four warp ends interlace in balanced four-end twill. The following four ends are reversed in the direction of the twill line. In herringbone, as in weft-reversed twill, observe the point of reversal or change from one direction to the other. The fifth end interlaces in opposite to the fourth. On the first pick, the fifth warp end is up; the fourth end lowered. Or, at the point of reversal, the first end of the new group interlaces in the opposite direction to the last end of the beginning group.

ends are woven two up, two down. The reverse, or break, causes alternate picks to interlace the warp in plain weave order. Short reversing of this kind creates a modified, less pronounced zigzag.

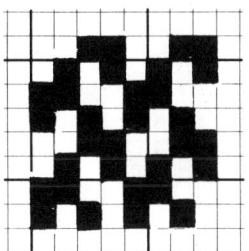

Fig. 134. Small herringbone twill.

Offset twill is made by breaking the twill line without reversing direction. Offset weaves have an unpronounced structure, adaptable in all-over projects. The break in these twills appears either in weft or warp direction. Intricate types may have a break in weft and warp in a single pattern.

Basic offset twill is similar to the reversed twill (*Fig.* 130). An offset example (*Fig.* 135) demonstrates a unit of four ends evenside twill offset to the right. The change is made after a unit of four is finished, as in regular twill. The last pick of a unit inter-

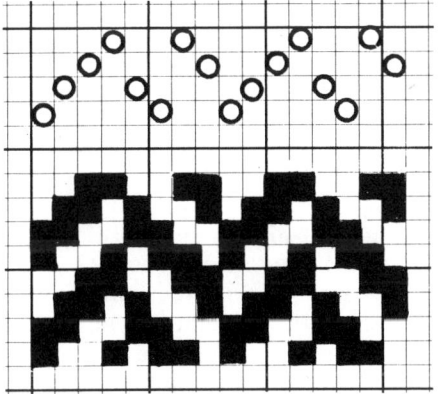

Fig. 133. Herringbone, evensided twill.

All warp-reversed twills require a change in threading heddles. The entering draw (*Fig.* 133) shows four ends threaded straight draw, alternating with four ends on shafts 2, 1, 4 and 3. In this threading arrangement, the warp ends that bind in the same way on each pick of a unit are put on the same shafts. Warp end 5 in this weave, for example, has the same interlacing as end 2, and both must be threaded on the same shaft.

The illustration (*Fig.* 134) is in an evensided or balanced twill, reversed every two warp ends, creating an all-over pattern. The

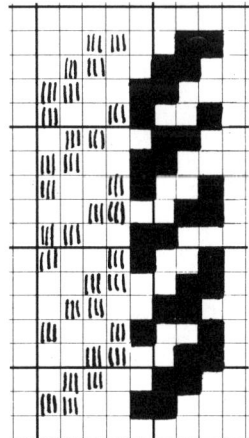

Fig. 135. Offset twill, weft direction.

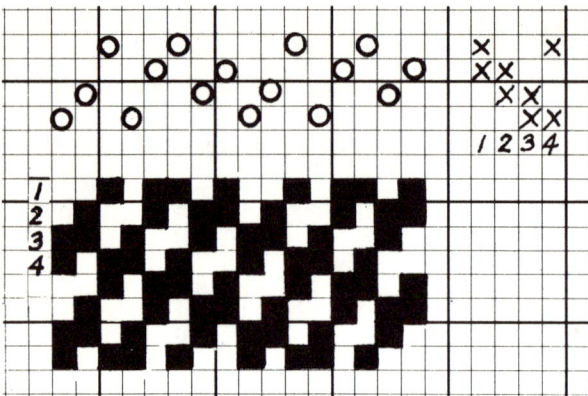

Fig. 136. Offset twill, warp direction.

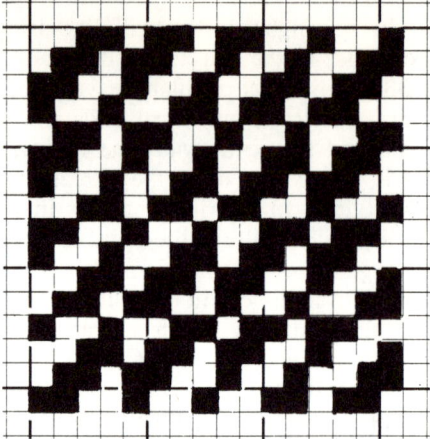

Fig. 137. Offset twill, combining both weft and warp direction.

laces in the opposite way from the following, or first pick, of the new unit. Thus, after each fourth weft, a break occurs. The weave repeats after sixteen picks and is straight-draw, four shafts.

An evenside twill, rearranged with broken diagonal in all-over pattern, is shown in *Fig.* 136. To construct, begin with a fundamental weave, as in all twill derivatives. Break up, or divide, the pattern after every two ends. The two-end groups repeat, as in basic evenside twill. Alternate two-end groups, however, may be any twill interlacing scheme of twos. In the illustration, warp ends one and two interlace as in regular evenside twill. Ends three and four are derived from ends four and one of the basic twill pattern.

Rearrangement from regular twill requires changes in threading, indicated in the illustration. Rotation in shaft-lifting, however, is in regular order: weft shafts 3 and 4 are lifted, then 2 and 3. In the third weft, shafts 1 and 2 are up; in the last pick, shafts 1 and 4.

By arranging basic twills in both warp and weft direction, original styles are produced. The illustration (*Fig.* 137) is a variation in which evenside twill is formed into new patterns by altering warp and weft rotations.

Zigzag twills resemble broken reversed twill. Diagonal lines slant in opposite directions at intervals. The zigzags may be lengthwise or horizontal across the cloth. In ordinary herringbone the pointed structure may also appear across the fabric.

Zigzag twill runs to the right for one unit (four ends), and then slants with two warp ends in the opposite direction (*Fig.* 138). The reverse slanting requires change in threading draft. The entering order follows the weave for four ends straight draw, from front to back shaft. The following two ends are straight-threaded from back to front.

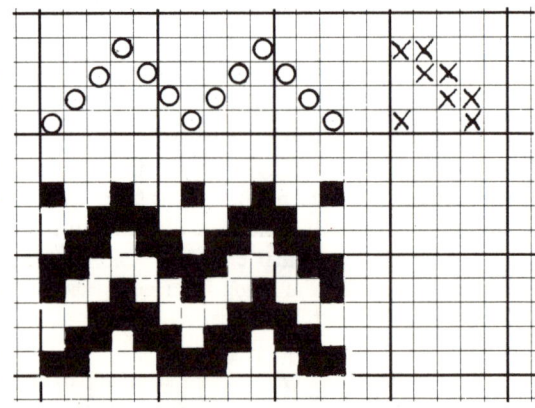

Fig. 138. Zigzag twill, warp direction.

WEAVES

Shafts are raised for zigzag weave in evenside twill order—1 and 2 up, 2 and 3 up, 3 and 4 up, 4 and 1 up.

Herringbone zigzags may be woven in balanced as well as unbalanced patterns. Size of zigzag depends on yarn density per inch. To construct a 2-inch herringbone of 20 warp ends per inch, thread the warp for twenty ends, one inch from front to back shaft (for left-to-right diagonal). Alternate with twenty ends for the opposite direction, from back to front shaft.

If the zigzag effect is to run lengthwise on the fabric, use straight draw. The twill line is reversed after a certain number of picks (*Fig.* 139). Slanting and size of herringbone may be as varied as in the warpwise style described above. Any basic twill may be used for a herringbone variation.

In another type of zigzag, the twill line is reversed at intervals in both warp and filling. The lines intersect at four points, forming diamonds. Variations of the diamonds are made by increasing the number of threads from point to point in warp and weft. Developments of weft twill diamond pattern are illustrated (*Figs.* 140, 141). The twill is the same in both of these patterns, but is given additional threads from point to point.

The illustration (*Fig.* 140) represents weft twill diagonal for four picks in one direction, followed by reverse. The illustration (*Fig.* 141) shows eight picks in one direction, and reverse. Adding more picks in one direction, the diamond is made increasingly larger than the style illustrated.

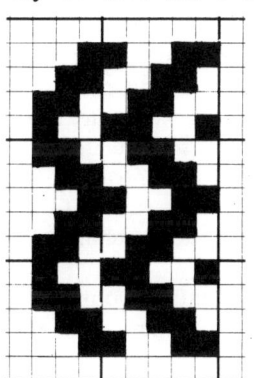

Fig. 139. Zigzag twill, weft direction.

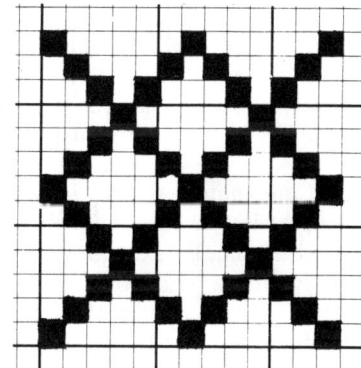

Fig. 140. Basic diamond twill.

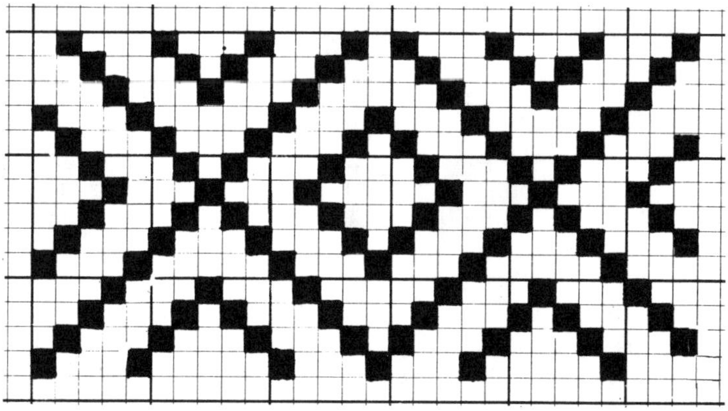

Fig. 141. Diamond twill elaborated.

Combination Weaves

Plain weave, twill, satin and their derivatives may be combined in other designs. A horizontal stripe consisting of two fundamental weaves (*Fig.* 142) is suggested as one of these. The first stripe is four picks—four-end weft twill slanting from left to right. The contrasting stripe has four wefts warp twill, slanting in reverse. The pattern is four shafts, straight draw.

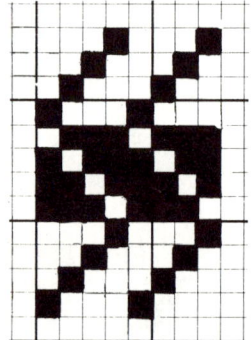

Fig. 142. Horizontal stripe, warp and weft twill alternating.

Combination weaves may be crosswise or lengthwise stripes, plaids or checks.

One simple example of cross stripe is plain weave with rib, in which basic weaves create texture contrast. The more extreme the two weaves, the more effective the surface of the textile in which they are combined. The illustration (*Fig.* 143) presents a flat plain weave area contrasted beside a

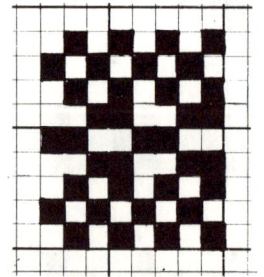

Fig. 143. Horizontal stripe, plain weave and rib alternating.

pronounced rib stripe. The next illustration (*Fig.* 144) shows an area of plain weave opposed to four-pick weft twill. The contrast of weaves, in this, are stronger than in *Fig.* 143 because of the diagonal accent between smooth and even plain weave.

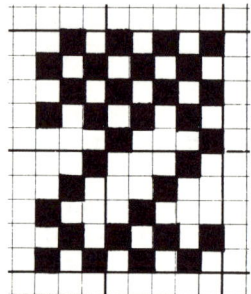

Fig. 144. Horizontal stripe, plain weave and weft twill alternating.

Care is taken in combination weaves at the meeting of the last pick of one weave with first pick of the following contrasting area. The last pick of plain weave area (*Fig.* 144) has even-numbered warp ends raised, while the first pick in the contrasting weft twill has odd-numbered ends raised. Careful joining of weaves preserves the character of each construction.

Weft and warp twill combinations achieve a high contrast of weave textures. The illustration (*Fig.* 142) is a draft showing the striking quality of light and dark areas. The joinings mentioned above are made especially clear in this example. The last row of weft twill has every fourth end raised. The following pick (first weft of new weave) shows the ends raised. These were hidden on the last, or adjoining, weft twill row.

Vertical striping is similar to cross stripe. Two or more weaves are combined in long stripes, with attention given to the joinings. Raised warp ends of the first and last threads in each weave are opposite to the hidden ends of first and last threads in the adjacent stripe. Contrasting warp interlacing preserves the character of each stripe construction. If the pair of adjacent threads (first and last in each stripe) does not break, the stripes become irregular in width, either the warp or weft floating across the dividing line.

A warp with weft twill stripe (*Fig.* 145) suggests this rule: The last and first warp end in each stripe interlaces in contrast. The lifted warp threads join the filling.

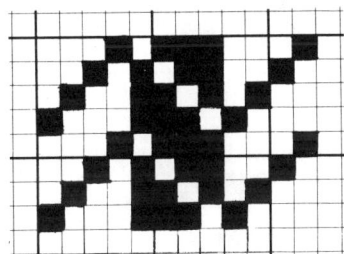

Fig. 145. Lengthwise stripe, warp and weft twill alternating.

In plain weave with rib stripe (*Fig.* 146) the break is not so perfect as the example in *Fig.* 145, but the close interlacing of plain weave prevents irregularity. Select suitable weaves for lengthwise stripes. For example, combine the interlacings in warp direction, noting similarity of number of warp and filling interlacings between each construction. If the patterns are similar in weave they will make up evenly.

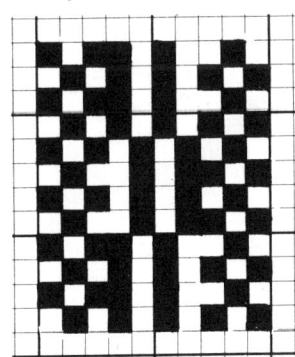

Fig. 146. Lengthwise stripe, plain weave alternating with rib.

A closely interlaced plain weave may be used with basket weave (3 up, 3 down), as illustrated (*Fig.* 147). These are dissimilar constructions. The warp ends in the basket weave interlace with the filling only four times in twelve picks. But, in the plain weave, warp and weft interlace twelve times during an equal number of picks. Contrast of interlacing prevents the picks in plain weave from being pressed closely against one another as in basket weave, where intersections are not so frequent. The more often warp and filling interlace, the more difficult the job of beating weft closely against the preceding pick.

Fig. 147. Plain and basket weave combined.

In *Fig.* 147 the easily sliding picks characteristic of basket design are shown. The warp ends in the plain weave are deflected from a straight line to a greater extent than in the basket area. The up-and-down moving, or take-up, of the warp sometimes gives a wrinkled, seersucker-like appearance to the fabric. Sometimes, for a special design purpose, this effect may be wanted. As a rule, however, close and loose weaves are not combined. Use of two beams on the loom will prevent irregularity, allowing each warp its proper tension.

Lengthwise stripes are often selected in designing decorative cottons, the smooth material being well adapted to bring out detail of weave. In wool, however, the weaves should be uniform, in order to control the effect of the rough fiber.

As in herringbone construction, lengthwise stripes usually demand special threading drafts, as well as the use of more than four shafts. The design shown (*Fig.* 145) requires eight shafts but each stripe is straight draw, four shafts for eight warp end changes.

By combining crosswise and lengthwise stripes in various quantities the weaver creates plaid. The ideas explained in the foregoing sections on stripes apply to this design. Weave patterns in plaid must break with each other along all lines of contact.

Examples of plaid—ideas for which are always enhanced by color—are suggested. Design, (*Fig.* 148) 2 up, 2 down (evenside), has a twill ground with plaid, or contrast, in basket weave using four shafts. Design (*Fig.* 149), with ribbed plaids, requires six shafts.

Small and large checks are designed in contrasting weaves in all types of fabric. Maximum effect is achieved by opposing constructions in weave and color.

Twill and satin are the best interlacings for this design. A warp and weft twill is shown in *Fig.* 150. The contrast is visual, or obvious, in the draft. When this pattern is made in one color, the structure of the alternate warp and weft squares creates a contrasting texture. When the warp is dark with light filling, there will be a tone as well as texture contrast. The warp twill checks have more warp (dark threads) on the surface, contrasting with the weft-effect squares, in which light filling is predominant. Pattern (*Fig.* 150) requires eight shafts, each stripe or group needing four shafts, straight draw.

The design in *Fig.* 150 may be changed, for example, by introducing a row of plain weave between each pick, or a row of rib weave may alternate with a row of squares.

Warp and weft satin weave are combined

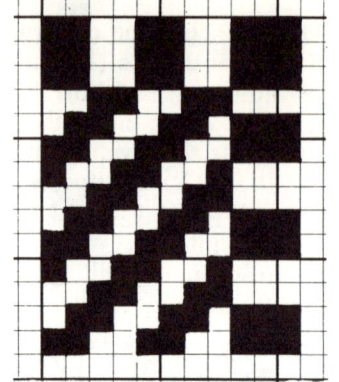
Fig. 148. Plaid, evensided twill and basket weave alternating.

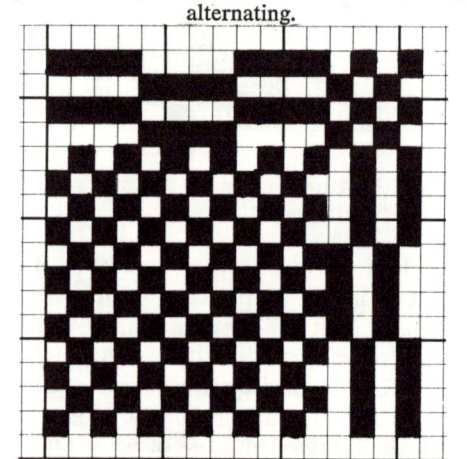
Fig. 149. Plaid, plain weave alternating with rib.

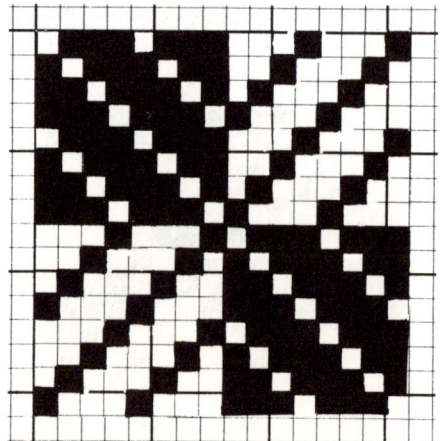
Fig. 150. Warp and weft twill check.

to form checks (*Fig.* 151). This five-end satin checkerboard has a first pick of satin weave filling stitches on the third warp thread (counting from left to right). The last weft is stitched on the third warp thread from right to left. In this arrangement each square of the same weave begins and ends by achieving a perfect break between warp and filling. The illustrated draft calls for ten shafts, each section straight draw.

Color Values in Relation to Weave

Geometric effects are created by combining warp and weft color arrangements specifically related to the weave. A plain weave, for example, may be transformed into upright and lengthwise stripes. A warp of dark and light alternating ends may have thin uprights when a dark weft is used in a shed of raised light ends. The light weft may be thrown when the odd-numbered ends are raised. The procedure, reversed, achieves crosswise lines: the darks raised and a dark filling required. When the light ends are up, light wefts are used (*Fig.* 152).

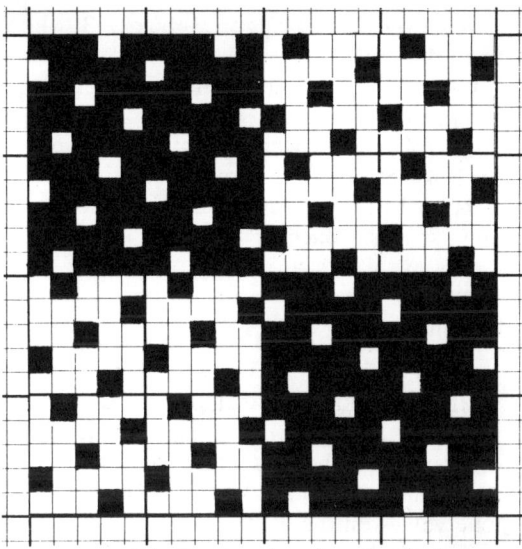

Fig. 151. Warp and weft satin check.

Fig. 152. Sampler of weave variations. Warp (left side) is 2 light and 1 dark. Right side of sampler is 3 light and 3 dark. White weft stripe separates samples.

An evensided twill of 3 black, 3 white warp and weft makes a step pattern. A basket weave may be transformed, through color arrangement, into a star design. A herringbone, following certain use of color, appears as dark net on white ground. All these subjects for basic color-and-weave study of hairline stripes, checks, birdseye and step motifs are illustrated.

Drafting color

Color, as well as weave, is marked on draft paper. Layouts include values of light and dark as they will appear in cloth. In order to conceive the value patterns, both warp and weft are marked in their respective tone values on the graph.

The illustration (*Fig.* 153, A and B) is a color layout of 1 dark, 1 light plain weave, alternating in warp and weft. Color drafting usually is begun with the entering draw. Fill in the dark square representing the first dark threaded end on the first shaft. The second, or alternating, light end on the second shaft will be shaded in the row above, as in the illustration. This process is continued until the fourth square is marked, and the unit of four ends is repeated.

A few rows below the entering draft, the plain weave is indicated by dots, or by thin lines. This is done lightly, so that later, when color values are superimposed on the weave, the interlacing or plain weave marks are not visible. On any vertical row of checks, near the left side of the weave, filling colors are designated. Black squares for first weft row, shaded for the second, or alternating lighter pick, are used. A red and blue pencil may be used in this work. Red will represent light tones. The blue pencil is reserved for darks.

Illustration 153B shows advanced steps. Fill in black squares for dark tones on top of dotted plain weave warp end raisers. First dark warp end runs from top to bottom over and under a pick. The second, and lighter, warp thread contrasts under first and over second weft, top to bottom. The second (last in the unit) is a light end, for which we designate warps on top of filling by shading the squares. When tone effects for the warp interlacings are completed, the weft is filled in.

Illustration 154 demonstrates completion of the draft, alternating dark and light horizontal lines. The wefts have been filled in, appearing in their respective values. Execute this final step in the graph by marking from left to right on the first row, in filling direction. The second and fourth light ends are down in this row, covered by a dark pick; therefore, the black weft squares are filled in. In the alternate weft, light-colored filling covers odd-numbered dark ends. Thus the whole row is shaded, using a red pencil.

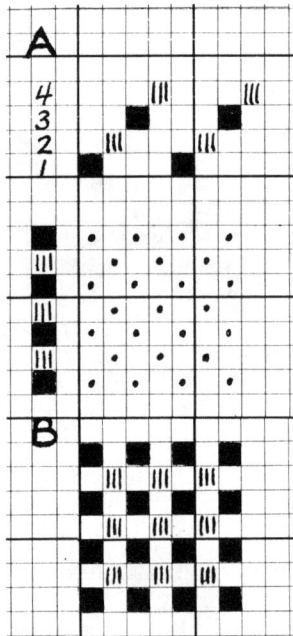

Fig. 153. Drafting for color. (A) Threading draft with dark and shaded checks indicating alternating dark and light color values. Dots show the plain weave interlacing. (B) Color value indication of the raised warp ends.

WEAVES

Hairline patterns consist of solid-color horizontal or vertical lines a thread wide. Examples are shown in *Figs.* 154, 155. The latter example is a color arrangement of 1 dark, 1 light, with the filling color reversed. Dark weft is used in a shed of raised light ends. The alternating lighter weft is entered when the darks are up.

By arranging weave and color, solid lines may be produced that are equal in width to two or more threads. Basket weave (*Fig.* 156) represents this idea. Color order in entering the yarns is alternately 2 dark, 2 light. The darks are on shafts one and two, the lighter yarns on harnesses 3 and 4. When the dark ends on shafts one and two are raised together, a light-toned double filling is inserted. For the next pick, in this construction, shafts three and four are lifted. The filling is a dark double-thread weft, forming wide upright lines. The pair of dark-toned ends, alternating with the lighter pair, transforms this basket weave into lengthwise stripe effect.

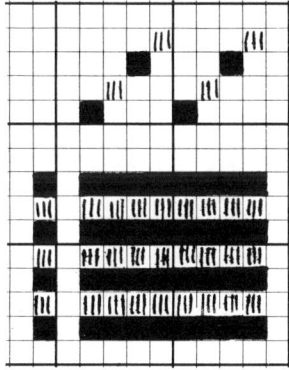

Fig. 154. Finished draft showing both warp and weft color values. Threading order (above), weft color order (at left), and block indicating complete effect—a hairline design of alternating dark and light.

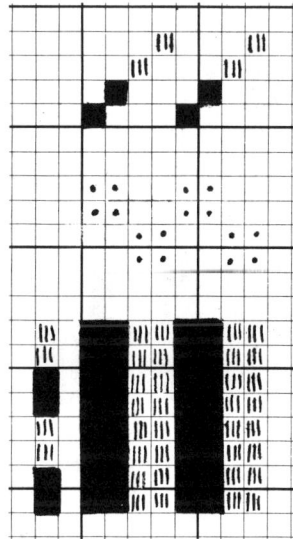

Fig. 156. Dark and light hairline, basket weave.

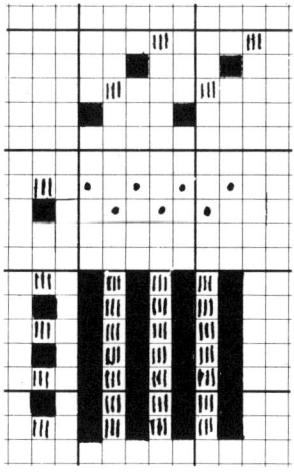

Fig. 155. Lengthwise dark and light hairline.

Ideal examples of color value in checks are found in log cabin and shepherd's check styles. In log cabin, a horizontal and vertical line combination, the warp layout is alternate dark and light for one or two inches. The reverse—one light, one dark for the alternating two inches—forms the squares. The illustration (*Fig.* 157) is a filling color arrangement similar to the warp layout. One or two inches, at first, are woven 1 dark, 1 light, forming an alternate row of horizontal and vertical structures. In the following order of picks or reversed checked row, a light and a dark complete the second row of checks. Log cabin is made on four shafts, straight draw.

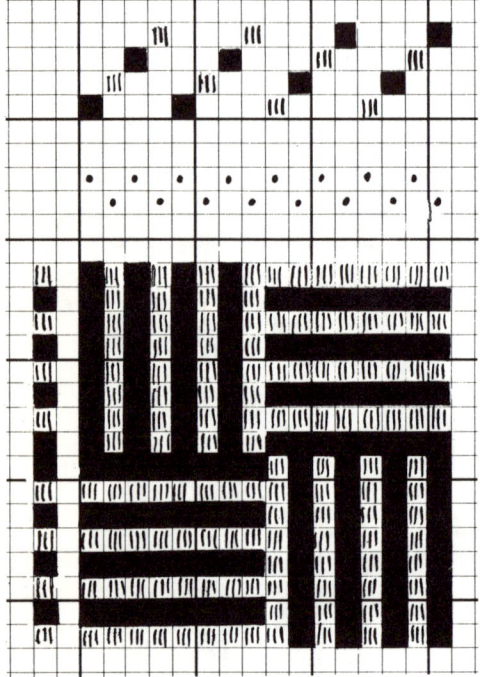

Fig. 157. Color value indication of plain weave checks.

Shepherd's check is a traditional motif in woolen suitings. Color distribution in the warp is alternately four dark, four light. The illustration (*Fig. 158*) shows the value effect. In this check use the same filling order as in the warp layout—four light, four dark, alternating in evensided twill. The pattern is made on four shafts, straight draw. On this warp original weaves and color values may be based.

A pattern in which the surface of the

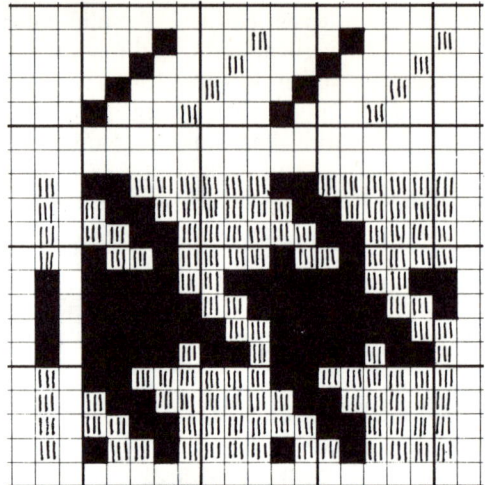

Fig. 158. Shepherd's check, evensided twill, in light and dark color.

cloth has distinct light or dark small flecks is usually called birds-eye. We find it in cotton and rayon, as well as wool. The illustration (*Fig.* 159) is the complete layout.

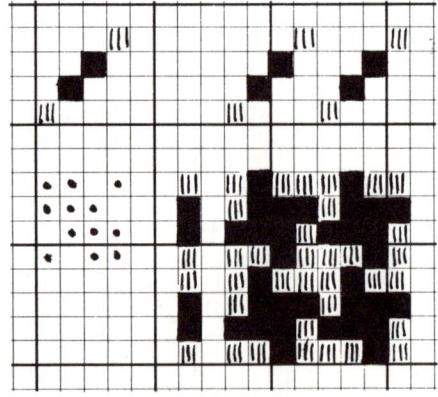

Fig. 159. Birdseye, evensided twill.

Warping in this pattern is two light, two dark, straight draw, entered on four shafts. The weft has the same order, but the weave is four-end warp twill.

Step patterns are simple stripes woven diagonally throughout the cloth, dark on light, or vice versa. Twill and its derivatives are ideal weaves in step design. The variation of tones is generally the same in warp and weft. This is illustrated in *Fig.* 160, in which ends and picks alternate one light, one dark, throughout an evensided four-end twill. The larger the color repeats the bolder the design.

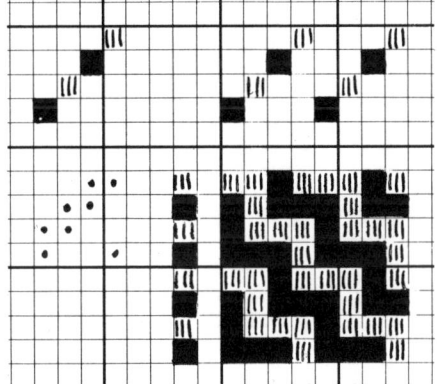

Fig. 160. Step pattern, evensided twill.

Honeycomb

Small sunken squares outlined by raised threads are called honeycomb, a design ordinarily seen in baby blankets, pot holders and hot plates. This weave can be used in making suitings and decorators' materials by employing special yarns and colors.

The honeycomb is the result of arranging groups of warp and weft floats combined with plain weave. Floating (non-intersecting) warp and weft create the raised frames around the squares. The sunken division is plain weave.

The illustration (*Fig.* 161) is based on zigzag diamond twill. The weft-float squares form raised horizontal outlines, with alternating squares having warp floats as vertical framework. The entering draw corresponds with the weave: four ends are threaded from front to back shaft, straight draw, with ends 5 and 6 reversed, back to front. The entering order is then repeated. The weaving or harness-raising order begins with single shafts. For the first pick, raise shaft four; second pick, shaft three; and for the third weft, two and four are lifted together. To make the last weft before reversing, lift shafts one, three and four. Then reverse the shaft-raising order, as in the threading draft (or third and second pick lifting order).

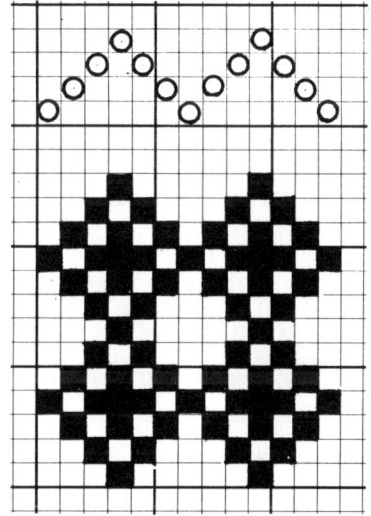

Fig. 161. Honeycomb, point threading.

For best effects in honeycomb weave, an even-numbered amount of ends should comprise the unit. It is possible to elaborate this weave by using units of eight, sixteen, or more ends depending on the project.

Lace, or mock leno

The mock leno weave creates open spaces, or lace-like effects. It is used for sheer drapery materials, shawls and fabrics requiring porous texture.

Either the warp or filling threads, in groups of three or more, are interlaced in bunches. One group of the yarns is separated from the other by contrast-interlacing of the last and first thread in each group. The sliding together, or bunching, of the groups is illustrated (*Fig.* 162), which shows that the first and last threads interlace alike in each group. The identical intersection of yarns 1 and 3 causes easy sliding. The center thread in each group floats over or under several yarns, depending on the group chosen. Four floating yarns alternate over and under three warp ends in the illustrated design. Its porous effect is created by plain weave—the last and first thread in each group.

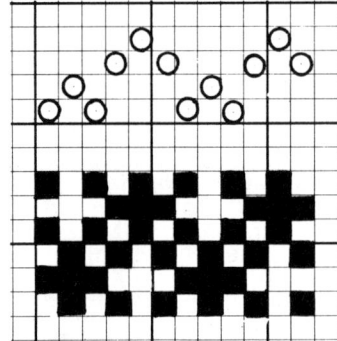

Fig. 162. Lace, or mock leno, 6 warp yarns threaded section draw.

The entering draft for the example is in sections, or groups: first end on shaft one, second on shaft two. End three interlaces in the same order as end one, therefore it is threaded on the first shaft. The next group is entered on shafts three and four. Warp end four is on the third shaft, and five goes through the heddle on shaft three. The last yarn of the unit, like thread four, is also entered on shaft three.

In lifting the harness in this project, raise one and four for the first pick and, for the following weft, three and four. The third pick, interlacing like the first, requires that one and four be lifted. Raise harnesses two and three for the next three picks, and then alternate with first and second shafts. This order is repeated, six wefts comprising the unit.

The illustration (*Fig.* 163) produces a mock leno with open, or lace, effect created by groups of three yarns. Sleying the threaded yarn through dents in reeds is usually a process independent of weave pattern.

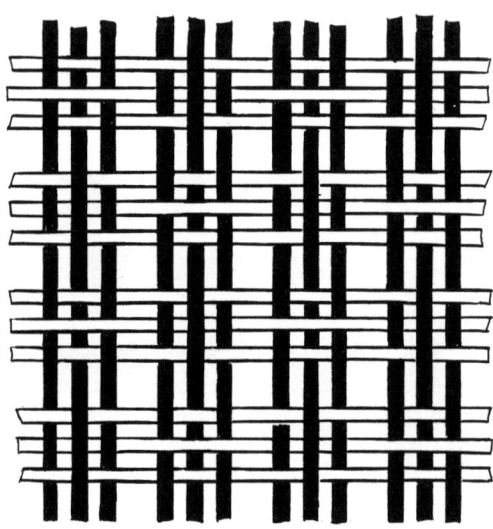

Fig. 163. Groups of three threads with intervening open space, main characteristic of lace weave, technically achieved by leaving unthreaded dents in the comb.

Twills, for example, may be dented either two or more per dent, depending on quality (density) of the cloth desired. Sleying (*Fig.* 163) relates to the specific weave.

As a rule, the three ends of each group are put in one dent. However, when fine yarns and reeds are used, separation between the groups is single-dented, only one thread per slit. Three or more ends in one dent should exactly fit for up-and-down shaft operation. Bunching threads closely in one dent holds them firmly together, making straight open spaces between groups. This sleying technique is characteristic in mock leno.

In planning an extremely porous fabric with large holes, dents are left empty between the groups of three or more ends. For example, mock leno (*Fig.* 163) could be sleyed three ends per dent, with two left out —this repeated throughout the cloth. In other variations, the order—three sleyed, two dents left out—is planned for one inch. The layout or composition thus continues with half-inch empty dents alternating with one-inch sleyed dents, creating a lengthwise sheer texture. The alternating dented and omitted areas produce lengthwise stripes. In the dented area (*Fig.* 163) warp and weft interlace, but the alternating stripe exposes weft only, since in this area no yarns are dented.

Mock leno is used with other weaves to create variety in sheer materials. Lengthwise striping may be designed with alternating plain and mock leno weave. Two-inch stripes in plain weave alternating with equal stripes in mock leno is an example. A more elaborate invention is large and small checks, one square in plain weave, the other in lace construction. The illustration (*Fig.* 164) is the scheme of this checked sheer fabric.

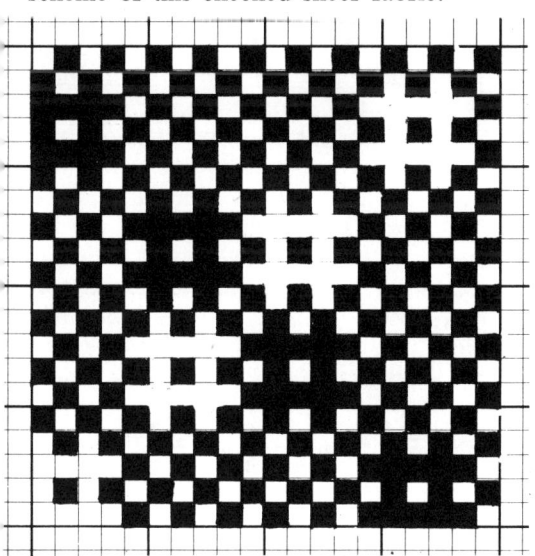

Fig. 164. Check variation in mock leno, or lace, weave.

Corded weaves

Corrugated effect in lengthwise and cross stripes is a popular construction. In the horizontal variety, the ribbed or raised stripes are derived from warp ends floating in back of the material. The alternating ends float, uninterlaced with weft, behind the raised stripe for 4, 6 or more picks. The remaining warp ends interlace in plain, or similar, weave. When the floating area is woven four or five wefts, the non-interlaced loose ends are raised and woven two or three picks. A basic draft for cross cord, shown in *Fig.* 165, depicts the construction.

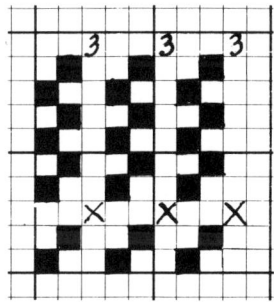

Fig. 165. Cross cord, every third warp yarn floating under 6 wefts.

In the illustration, every third warp end floating under six picks forms the corded or ropelike structure. The hidden ends appear on the surface, or top, of the recessed weft in each unit. The alternating two ends interlace in plain weave, but are under the recessed pick (x-marked in the draft). This order is repeated throughout the cloth.

Two or four recessed wefts may be used to create pronounced grooves, especially when fine yarns are employed for recessing, with heavy filling for the cord (*Fig.* 166). The alternating ends, in this pattern, float under four wefts while the rest interlace in plain weave. Picks five and six, which form the recess, are in plain weave. The following group, which makes the cord, has odd-numbered ends floating, the remaining thread interlaced in plain weave. This unit of twelve picks is repeated throughout.

Fig. 166 is made on four shafts, straight draw. Alternate two and four with one and three. And, for the last four picks in the unit, alternate shafts two and four. In the interlacing of the recessed picks, note that when one cord is finished, shafts two and four are raised. Also note that, with the alternating cord, the first recess interlaces with odd-numbered ends.

Fig. 167. Section of weaving: black dots are warp, with over and under weft, and floating weft passing under 6 warps. The draft of this is shown in the following plate, a design for warp cord.

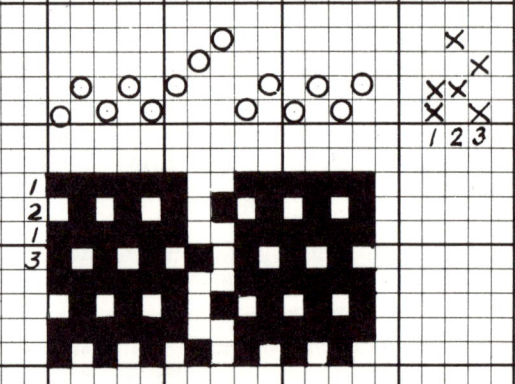

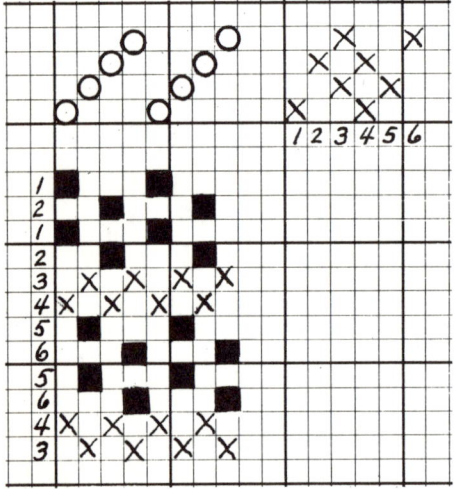

Fig. 166. Cross cord with alternating warp yarns passing under 4 wefts, separated by two rows of plain weave. Threading order is given above draft, with warp lifting order at right.

Fig. 168. Warp cord with threading and shaft-lifting drafts. Two warp yarns are recessed, forming grooves.

Six ends are entered straight on shafts one and two, the two alternate threads on harnesses three and four. Throughout the project raise shafts one with two, alternating with plain weave.

In lengthwise cords, woven without recessed threads, each pick floats alternately on the back and interlaces with the warp of adjacent cords. In one cord the weft will be on the back, and in the next will interlace on the face. The order is reversed on the following pick. This pronounced cording technique is illustrated in cross-section (*Fig.* 169) and in draft (*Fig.* 170). Each stripe

Vertical stripes, or warp cords, are made by wefts floating on the back under four or more ends. The picks come to the surface and cross one or two picks of plain weave. The warp ends, under which the picks float, are pressed upward forming an arch. The weave is represented in cross-section (*Fig.* 167) and in draft (*Fig.* 168). The raised stripe has six ends. Floating picks pass under these and are plain woven on two warp threads. The draft is executed on four shafts.

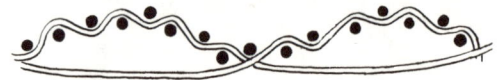

Fig. 169. Section of weaving: Over and under weft with floating weft passing under 8 warps, illustrating the following draft or warp cord.

is made with eight ends in plain weave on alternating picks, while the other floats under the cloth.

Back filling and double cloth

Customarily used in industry as an economy in making cloth thicker and heavier, the weave known as back filling is seldom employed by handweavers. Disregarding the fact that poor yarns generally are used in back filling, good use can be made of the technique, weaving the hidden picks in a color that contrasts with the surface.

The surface, therefore, will be in one color, the reverse (back filling) in another. Two constructions also may be used: the face in plain weave, for example, and the back in 3-up, 1-down twill. Back filling may also be an interlacing of all the warp threads with the filling, face as well as back. And there is a back-filling of another type in which a separate set of warp ends is used.

Back filling is drafted as follows: Mark the weaving order of face and back picks on graph paper, face picks alternating with back filling. The face weave is drafted first, alternate rows of graph checks being reserved for the back filling, which is noted last.

The illustration (*Fig. 171*), which is a diagram of back weave drafting, represents a pattern with surface of 1-up, 2-down twill, the back interlacing in reverse, 2-up, 1-down. The picks are alternately woven—one face, one back. This pattern is threaded on four shafts, straight draw.

Illustration 172 is plain weave on the surface with back filling of 3-up, 1-down twill, woven pick and pick (one face, one back).

For smooth and clear cloth surface the weft yarns, top and back, should be of equal size. If the back filling is in coarse thread and the top in fine yarn, the face of the cloth will be uneven. Thick back filling prevents

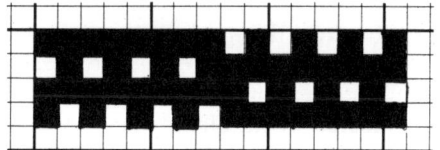

Fig. 170. Warp cord without grooves.

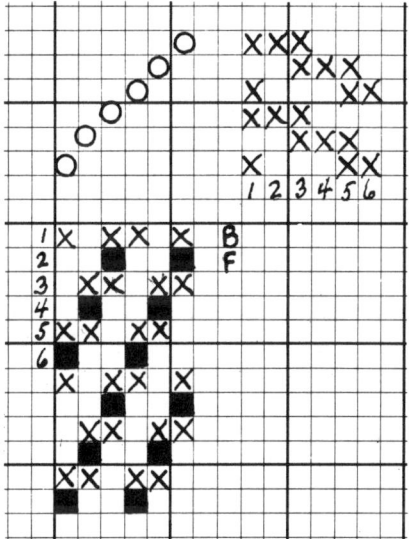

Fig. 171. Back filling of 1 up and 2 down twill, the x-marks indicating backfilled rows, which show on the reverse of the material and make a double-face cloth. Threading and shaft-lifting at top of plate.

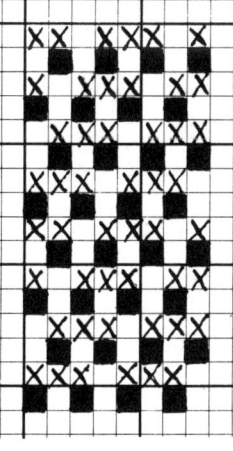

Fig. 172. Backfilling with plain weave surface, reverse of cloth 3 up and 1 down twill. This is made on four shafts.

top wefts from lying close together. But if the weaver desires to create marbleized and irregular design effects in the surface of the cloth, coarse back filling may be used to advantage. In using heavy back filling yarns, however, the wefts are usually woven in a ratio of two face wefts to one back, or even three face wefts to one.

When top filling in back weave is woven with long floats, the stitchers for the back should be as near as possible and opposite the center of the face filling float. The stitchers for back filling, however, should occur where the back weft is covered by adjacent filling threads.

Most weaves lend themselves to face and back filling combinations. The interlacings do not have to be basic weaves. The surface in *Fig.* 173, for example, is pointed or zigzag twill, the back filling interlacing in six-end warp twill.

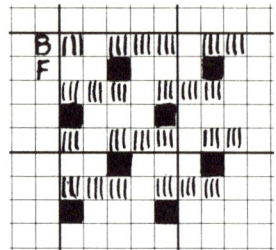

Fig. 174. Draft for tube of double cloth in plain weave. (B) back of cloth, (F) front, or face.

Illustration 174 is a plain weave tube of double cloth. The next illustration (*Fig.* 175) is a line drawing of the two layers on the loom. When this construction is warped and woven 1 dark, 1 light, the face fabric will be solid dark plain weave, the back material light, as indicated in *Fig.* 175. A

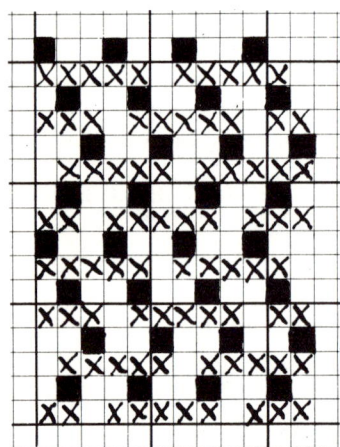

Fig. 173. Backfilling with zigzag surface, 6-end warp twill forming on the reverse.

A complex weave, called double cloth, is developed from back filling. Double cloth is two fabrics, a top and bottom layer woven separately on one warp. The double textile is stitched together at intervals. When double cloth is made without stitching face and

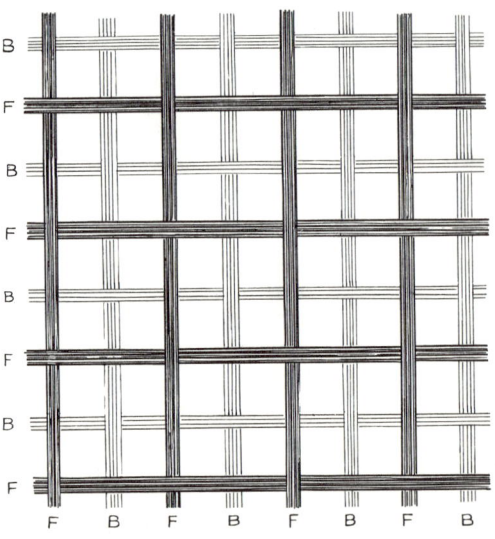

Fig. 175. Yarn interlacing for tube of double cloth in plain weave. Ruled lines present top layer, shaded lines indicate back layer, showing on the reverse, or inside of the tube of cloth.

double cloth stitched along one selvage only is illustrated in *Fig. 176*. When unfolded, it is twice as wide as the loom. The filling order in this design is two picks face, alternating with two for back.

There are yet more elaborate double cloths in twill, satin and other weaves. A weaver who studies and masters only a few of the interlacings described in this chapter will have technical knowledge sufficient to create an infinite number of original patterns varied and enhanced by color arrangement.

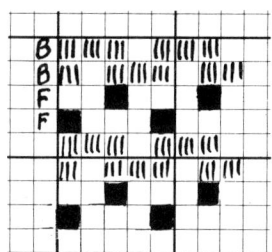

Fig. 176. Draft of double cloth stitched along one selvage, a device by which 40-inch cloth may be woven on a 20-inch loom. (BB) two rows of back filling and (FF) two rows of front, alternating.

Part IV. Design

A CRAFTSMAN'S work is always concerned with technical and esthetic values. He considers raw material in relation to the use of his fabric. Designers depend not only on idea but on self-knowledge and skill to realize the finished fabric. Weavers, like potters and cabinet-makers, prove their ingenuity artistically and, at the same time, answer practical demand.

It is not enough to learn fundamental weaves and do them on a loom. We must look for and see specific character and structure in weaves. With time and experience, the weaver develops a vocabulary of interpretations. A basic close weave, a diagonal or twill, will produce a practical cloth when made in the right density. Yet the twill is an ornament and can be used for expressive effect, as well as wearing quality. The diagonal line may be fine or thick, or it can be changed into small and large zigzags.

The elements in weaving are yarn, weave and color. The natural physical properties of yarn suggest usefulness, but yarns also have character. Degrees of softness in wool and luster in silk constitute textures. Thread, too, has volume or shape—fine, heavy, and irregular.

Density is one of the principal considerations in structure. Sometimes we may group threads close together in stiff, ribbed cloth, or, with very fine yarn, create opaqueness. By using open with closed areas in a textile surface, we obtain rhythm, a composition property.

Qualities without number may be achieved in yarns and weaves in natural tones alone. But usually color is incorporated in the design—subtle harmonies, brightness and contrast—and affects the use of all the elements.

The character of a textile is found equally by touch and sight and each cloth surface has its own visual-and-tactile value, or essence. The life of a woven fabric depends on the all-over disposition of the smallest particles in its structure. Cloth textures are hard, soft, rough, smooth, shiny, fluffy or embossed. In the warp threads, as well as the weft, variety, or composition, is created by alternating heavy with fine, nubby with plain, and smooth with rough.

Pattern in weaving is the graphic arrangement of lines resulting in stripes, checks or plaids. The motifs may be evenly distributed or combined in many ways. One example would be a material of equal stripe widths, whereas another may be composed of wide and narrow.

Since the weaver works for an expression in his fabric that will suit the intended use of the material, his foresight as a creator is what distinguishes him as a designer and inspires even his most experimental weaving. A clothing fabric, for instance, usually calls for a composition different from drapery. Some textiles can allow stronger color schemes than others, depending on the environment in which it will appear or be worn.

A designer makes his vision of a fabric become a tangible reality. He works through all the elements which produce a woven fabric to realize his plan.

Yarn

Raw material is a primary source of design inspiration. The yarns we use should interest us because of their origin and natural fiber characteristics, their twist and construction.

The weaver is interested first of all in the natural surface of a yarn, the qualities it suggests. The look of wool, for instance, is soft, dull, sometimes even heavy, and radiates warmth. Mohair and alpaca, while similar to wool, have more sheen. Where a designer is hoping to weave an extremely light and soft fabric, he will study fine yarns, those, for example, composed of angora rabbit hair or lustrous pure silk. Generally, as in the case of silk, appearance, rather than physical property, will be the main attraction. But, besides being luxurious, silk is a strong fiber, and has more serviceable uses than its mere surface suggests.

Weavers who make a point of studying fiber qualities discover new design purposes in them. It is the individual's seeking which finds original qualities and uses in fibers. You will note that cotton, in its raw stage, is dull and fluffy. It has none of the warm, heavy look found in wool. To the light, thin and airy characteristics of cotton, the weaver will add aspects he personally discovers in the material. In linen thread he will observe the quality of stiffness and be able to feel and see the source of the fiber in the dry stalks of a plant. Likewise, he will be able to see back into the natural source of glossy pineapple and hemp filaments. But some qualities the weaver-designer can realize only through technical information and study. He must know, for instance, that the glosses in linen and rayon fibers are added by process and chemicals and that they are not inherent in the basic substance. In short, as far as the weaver is willing to search, he will discover new sources in the yarn fibers themselves.

Analysis of surface effects of yarns and their fibers usually is immediately followed by respect for their construction. The twist, or composition, of yarn is of two main classes: plain or straight yarn, and irregular or novelty constructions. The straight threads are traditional and composed of a variety of twists and plies in one fiber. The degree to which a yarn is turned, or twisted, and the number of plies or strands in a yarn, determine much of its character. The size of a thread, or number of its plies, is, of course, a quantitative consideration. It is the twisting of yarn that should interest us in the study of yarn quality. Even when the raw material is soft, hard twisting will make it stiff and change the surface of the basic fiber. In very tightly twisted yarn, the turning

DESIGN

structure is almost invisible. The number of turns per inch governs the tightness or hardness of a thread.

When warp and filling are composed entirely of loosely twisted cotton, a smooth and dull appearance results in the cloth. For a stiffer, more structural effect, use a harder twist thread (*Fig.* 177). Thus movement in design is achieved by merely combining various twists of the same fiber in warp and weft. And this is a reliable way to achieve texture without employing novelty yarns or complex weaves. Yarns of different twist may be simply spaced, or distributed throughout warp and weft, forming designs as various and elaborate as desired.

One example would be a warp made of five or six soft-twisted threads alternating with two harder yarns to create a pattern of vertical lines in a monotone cloth. The

changes, or variations, possible in weaving in a single straight thread are further varied by employing threads of different sizes, or ply. The weaver can achieve a decided all-over pattern simply by alternating one thick and one fine-ply yarn at short intervals. The greater the spaces or difference in yarns, the greater the contrast in the resulting design. For example, one inch of heavy loosely-twisted cotton can be alternated in a stripe design with an inch of fine cotton thread of hard twist.

Combining different twists offers variety in any type of fabric, but is a most effective technique for sheer materials. In sheer or open cloth there are many possibilities of revealing yarn structure, since warp and weft are loosely interlaced. In net fabrics, the threads keep their character much more individually than in close weaves.

Imagine a warp of fine threads—six or seven closely grouped in one dent, with spaces omitted. The filling yarn will be the only effect in the omitted areas. Combine, for instance, a loosely twisted spun rayon of natural color with a harder twist of the same color and material to create variety through contrast of shiny and dull and to give an illusion of space. The shiny spun rayon attracts the eye more than the thin, hard twist and the spaces which the thin yarn leaves create an open effect.

Rhythm in a fabric does not only come from the contrast of dull with shiny, or from various twist combinations. It comes also from the volume or shapes in yarns (*Fig.* 178). Here again are endless design suggestions. Alternating heavy with fine yarn, or grouping the yarns in either regular or irregular spaces, results in relief cloth of thick and thin areas—a typical textile form. By crossing the areas with thick and thin weft, plaids and checks are made. The yarn makes the effect.

Contemporary weavers do not rely only on

Fig. 177. Weave designers discover and invent textures and contrasts in other materials than yarn. Here, reeds are combined with moss in a study of stiff and soft tactile values. *Lili Blumenau Weaving Workshop student work. Photo, Rudy Bleston.*

straight yarns. There is a much wider yarn choice for weavers today than in other centuries. Modern straight and novelty, or irregular, yarn provides the weaver with a constantly renewed variety of fibers.

A designer working with irregular yarns considers two ideas. He uses the yarns in contrast with straight threads; or, after studying their qualities, may transform them into an entirely new appearance. A length-

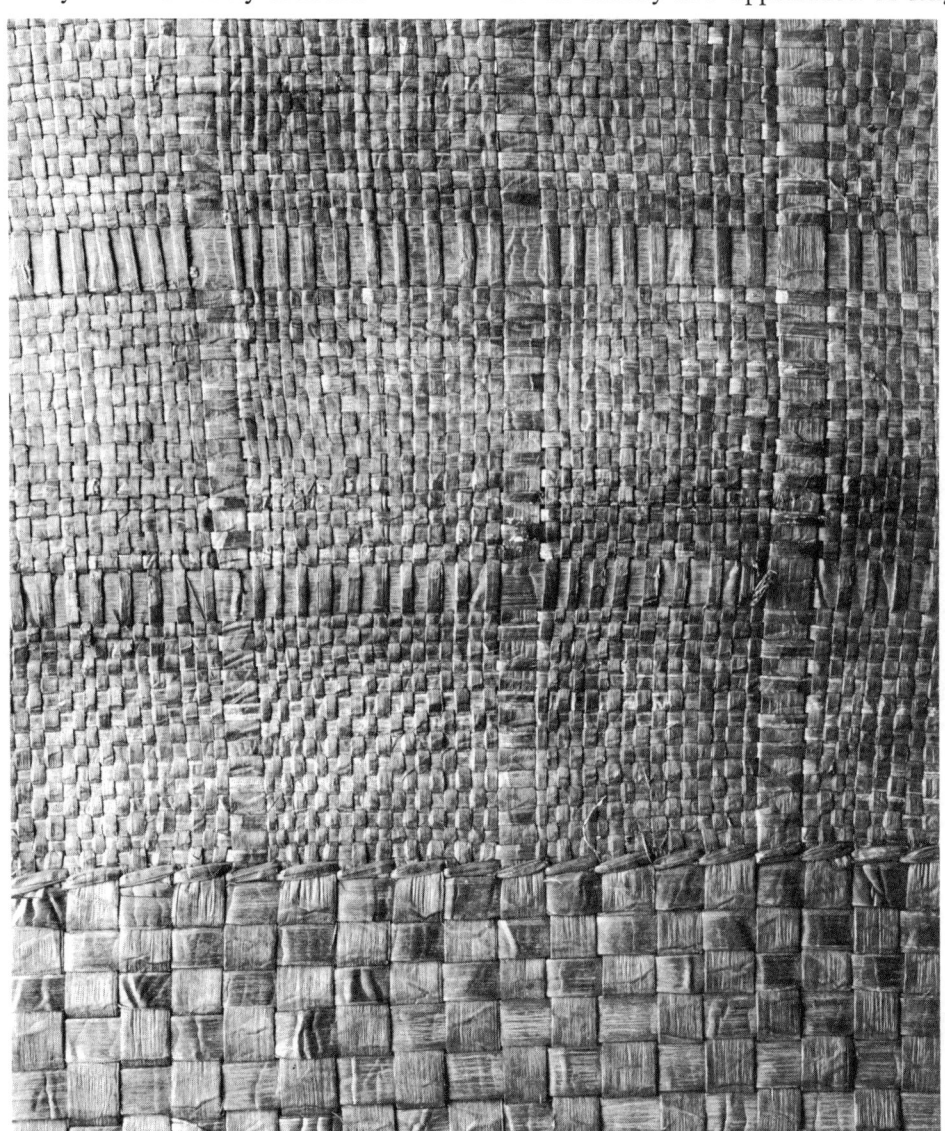

Fig. 178. Detail of a mat by American Indians of the Northwest, created by use of narrow and wide materials. Rhythm in plaid weaves in one color is produced by variation of heavy and fine yarns. *Smithsonian Institution.*

wise rib, alternated with filling of one plain yarn and one ratine, will produce lengthwise texture lines. Or, in a more varied composition, you may choose several types of straight yarn combined with flake and ra-

ratine is an effective thread to use with straight yarn in a warp layout, if the weave is appropriate: for example, two straight darks and two light ratines may alternate in the warp, and a filling consisting of straight dark

Fig. 179. A table mat, in which marble effect is obtained by using irregular, as well as varied, yarns—soft wool, stiff linen, and grass, in light and dark color values. *Jack Lenor Larsen, Inc., Designer.*

tine. The grouping in this kind of warp layout will make the weave, or weft, secondary —its purpose being only to hold the cloth together.

For heavy and furry effects, the natural curl of loop yarn offers the right means. Loop yarns are also used in sheer materials to create thin, fibrous surfaces. Heavy cotton

thread interlaced in basket weave, developing a crisscross ornament. Other weaves and other filling combinations will alter the appearance of the fancy thread in this warp. If an evensided twill is crossed with two light ratines and two dark straight threads, a ropelike effect on a dark ground will result.

With flake and nub threads there are fur-

108 THE ART AND CRAFT OF HAND WEAVING

Fig. 180. White Lines, 1942, painted by I. Rice Pereira, has well defined surface textures. Painting is a valuable source of study for weavers. *The Museum of Modern Art, New York. Gift of Edgar Kaufman, Jr.*

ther possibilities. The flake construction is beautiful and often looks like handspun yarn. In corded weaves, flake yarn increases the cord, or relief effect, but in transparent fabrics maintains its original character. Nub yarns in wool are widely used for suitings and are especially liked in mixed colors. A brown tweed fabric with yellow and red specks is an example of a nub yarn. Although the effect comes through color, it is the type of yarn itself which provides the means.

Very useful novelties are those in which bicolored threads or two raw materials are combined. A black and white twisted yarn will produce marble effects in weaving. And, if a novelty woolen yarn is twisted together with fine straight silk, highlights will appear in a cloth of contrasting dull surface. Any fancy yarn may be used as a design element, but must be related to technical values, weave, and intended purpose.

Weave Construction

Each weave has its own character. To know how each is woven is necessary as technique. To understand weaves, first discover their appearance and language. Textile making is the search for the right weave to carry out an idea.

A basic weave does not make an original cloth. The fabric is created by an interpretation and conversion of a basic weave. Take an analogy from painting. The painter begins with a visualization of his idea of a particular flower or person which he wants to realize in paint on canvas. Flowers, if they are tulips, are only tulips, just as plain weave is only plain weave, an impersonal, general pattern. In his picture, however, the tulips will be a new form of the flower, as seen and created by him. The same proposition confronts the weaver in transforming a weave.

Just as the painter acquaints himself with forms in nature, the weaver learns all he can about fundamental weaves. He will see that plain weave is an all-over structure when the warp and weft are made of the same yarn. He will notice that the appearance of the plain weave is even, because an equal amount of yarn is distributed over a square inch over both warp and weft. But when he uses a thicker filling than warp, the plain weave's appearance will change. The crossings or stitches formed by the individual warp yarns become longer and more pronounced, and the thick wefts make ribbed crosslines.

We see that this change comes about through different warp and weft distribution. If a warp of medium yarn, grouped 20 threads per inch for plain weave, is used with a filling of the same amount in the same space, an even surface is realized. The warp and weft appear in equal proportions. For cross-rib structure variation with a heavier yarn, there will be fewer wefts to the inch. The idea may be exaggerated by taking a fine warp and a ropelike thread for filling. For other variations, alternate fine and heavy yarns. Here, the individual warp threads will alternate between long and short stitches, whereas the filling will be an alternation of heavy and fine lines.

When plain weave, per inch, has twice as much filling as warp yarn, the result is an effect of ribs running the length of the cloth. This, too, can be varied according to choice — heavy or thick ribs with narrow, in all kinds of spacings. Historically speaking, the rib idea was invented when tapestry or figure weaving began. The warp yarns in early rib weave were concealed. The weft colors were distinct, which is essential in tapestry. As soon as the warp threads show, the color of the filling changed in relationship to the color of the warp, whereas in the lengthwise ribs we see the colors unified in solid planes.

Basket weave is a checkerboard. The

Fig. 181. Upholstery fabric of twill and plain weave check-forms, separated by cross rib. One check is weft twill, the other shows the black warp. *Lili Blumenau Design. Photo, Rudy Bleston.*

smallest checks are produced when side-by-side warp and weft threads interlace alternately. For large checks, a greater number of yarns are intersected in the same way. Equal checks, large or small, create evenness and simplicity when used alone. When they are combined, a more dynamic design develops. Basket weave is the simplest means for creating bold color contrasts. A light warp with dark filling produces highly relieved light checks against dark.

The twill weaves are linear ornaments. Although the diagonal of a twill may be only in one direction—right to left, or vice versa, across the fabric—the directions of twill lines can change the structural movement in a pattern. Zigzag twill can be either horizontal or vertical, as in herringbone.

Ornamental content in a weave may be achieved by other means than repeating the same motif. Rhythmic pattern is obtained by several different motifs or weaves arranged in continuity. By grouping and composing weaves, we arrive at new ideas and original constructions. The basic weave constructions are already invented, but every weaver is confronted anew with problems of how to use them artistically.

A simple combination use of plain weave and twill in various orders could be as follows: two rows woven in plain weave alternating with a unit of evensided twill, or stripes of warp with weft twill. In the first type the contrast between the two weaves is not so strong as in the twill combination. Proportionately speaking, in the plain weave and evensided twill, there is as much warp as filling; whereas in the warp twill the lengthwise structure is pronounced. Horizontal stitches appear, as contrast, in the weft. If you weave this last example on a light warp with dark filling, two stripes will be made—one with dark background and light diagonals, the other with light background and dark lines.

From these two examples we get an idea of the working procedure for transforming weaves into an all-over design. In the plain weave with twill, the effect is from the weave combination. But, in the stripe example of warp with weft twill, we have weave as well as color contrast. The knowledge of these possibilities prepares us when confronted with plans to create strong contrasts or subdued values in a fabric.

Weaves range from simple to dynamic expressions. When the weaver emphasizes color or yarn harmonies, the choice of weave often

Fig. 182. Decorative material with small geometric motif formed by combining two different weave constructions. *Jack Lenor Larsen, Inc., Designer.*

is secondary. Weave, in fact, can diminish effect. Confusion in a design may be the result of putting equal emphasis on all elements. A fabric of heavy and fine yarns in dramatic color combinations does not need a bold structure, such as a diamond or an irregular zigzag.

However, if emphasis is all on weave, with yarn and color neglected, one may discover a lack of artistic form. The weave becomes merely graphic and looks more printed than woven. One may learn to avoid this from textiles of earlier centuries. The Peruvian and Egyptian weavers had an intuitive knowledge of composition, yarn, color and proportion. We can imitate their approach in experimental work of our own. The weaver who knows and sees variety in warp and weft interlacing enriches his weaving vocabulary. He finds forms which stimulate his inventiveness and widen his range.

Color

Color is the supplementary agent of interlacing and yarn. In some textiles the interest is in yarn composition and weave construction, but there are many cases where color is the predominant feature.

Color sense in some people is highly developed—their choice and judgments in it are intuitive. Other people are less sensitive to it and not much affected by disharmonies. But no matter how developed the sense of color or how much the other elements in weaving attract us, color is indispensable in weaving.

Like weaves, colors have character, but gain more meaning and value by the way in which they are related. Seeing and feeling color is the preparation for disciplined use of it. We have no theoretical outline of the use of color, but we can get valuable information by experiment, study and practice. We can go beyond the accidental use of color.

The source of color is light without which there would be no visible color, shape or texture to objects. Our eyes receive intricate reflections of light waves and transfer their image for recognition and use to the brain. The unit of colored light which man has adopted for his convenience in study is called the solar or prismatic spectrum. The order of the spectrum was observed in nature, for example, the rainbow which has six divisions: red, orange, yellow, green, blue, and violet. There are infinite gradations of these hues, closely related, between each of the basic colors. Perception of a hue is based on its wave length. The longer waves of light are called warm tones; the shorter ones, cool. But when all light rays are combined we see white or achromatic light. Our sight of color depends on two visual sensations—chromatic (with hue) and achromatic (without hue).

The various colors, red, green, or blue, have values and intensities. Color varies from light to dark. Value is the word used to indicate the amount of light a surface reflects. White is above and beyond the color range, or spectrum, and black is below it. All color tones, chromatic and achromatic, fall between. To speak of a color's purity—intensity—we mean that neither black nor white nor any neutral tone has been added. A pure red, for example, cannot be reduced to a neutral shade without weakening the pure color's intensity.

In weaving, colors are seldom used alone, but usually in combination. The tone of a color—its dimension, or value, hue, and intensity—changes with its use. There is a complete relativity between tones in a composition. Influence of one color on another depends not simply on their color qualities but on the quantity, or space, each color occupies. A bright green weft that looks subdued in a grey warp in plain weave will be luminous in weft twill. The influence which colors have on each other side-by-side is so strong at times that the apparent color of the yarn is completely changed in the woven structure. By learning and seeing these conditions, we can produce desired effects.

Colors are put together either in monochromatic or polychromatic contrast. A monochromatic contrast consists of two or more values, or intensities, of a single color: two shades of red, or, for another example, a brilliant green with a neutral shade. When differing colors are combined, a polychromatic effect results—as light blue with dark green; or light red with orange and purple.

The transformation of the colors when they are combined is an important study. When we choose two colors that are similar in value and intensity, we discover that they influence each other very little. A light red next to a light orange on a neutral pale grey warp does not cause much change between the tones. But a striped warp, one inch black alternating with one inch white, using medium grey filling, will undergo many changes. The same grey will look dark in the white area and appear light against the black stripe. We can discover similar types of changes in one-colored warps. All colors look darker and deeper in white warps, white having intense light and capacity to overpower other tones. On a black warp, however, the colors look brilliant and light. When a weaver wants to keep the weft tones fairly normal, however, he generally chooses a neutral or grey warp.

In study of hue contrast one encounters all kinds of changes. The difference between hues is qualitative, whereas the value changes are quantitative. We can say that we are guided in hue contrasts by temperature change. If you put an area of green next to an area of bright blue, the green will turn warm and yellowish. But the same green, close-up with a warmer tone, a red or yellow, will appear cool and much less colorful.

In intensity contrast there are all kinds of relative changes. By combining analogous tones, such as brilliant red with reddish-orange, the law of increased difference is evoked. The more intense, objective tones, the brilliant red, for example, look more intense than they are, whereas the reddish-orange appears to be quite neutral. When complementary and near-complementary colors are contrasted in this way, the contrasts become even more complex, contrasts too strong to look at. A well-known example of this juxtaposition is red-orange next to bright blue-green—tones that are approximately complementary and full of intensity. To use such great contrasts successfully, either drastically subordinate the area of one tone so that the other dominates, or reduce the intensity of one of the colors. Another way is to separate both the strong colors by a neutral shade.

The various colors which change in content or dimension affect the area they occupy. When we use a light color next to a darker, in equal amounts, the light area will appear large and the dark, small (*Fig. 183*). However, by combining warm and cool colors, the warm sections appear larger than the cool.

Psychological factors also influence color perception. We usually sense in reds and yellows warmth and excitement; in blues and greens, calm and cool effect. Cool tones recede from the eye, whereas the warm ones have a tendency to expand and advance toward it. Hues also are subjective. Red is thought aggressive and startling. A great many people do not like orange because the warmth and vibrancy are overstimulating. Generally, however, people like to be surrounded by green tones. These—unconsciously associated with nature and growth—produce the most natural reactions. Violet and purple, symbolic colors of authority, respect and dignity, are not common, but ap-

Fig. 183. Areas of exactly the same size, but light color on dark at left appears larger than dark on light, at right.

peal to most people because of their rarity and distinctiveness.

In time we learn to control emotional reaction to color as we gain knowledge of how to employ it. The evidence of the senses can be used constructively only through knowledge. Most color experience remains on the level of sensation, but knowledge comes when perceptions have been analyzed and formed into useable ideas. Consciousness of color effect and awareness of its influence is a necessity in the layout or planning of textiles.

A common color problem is found in the attempt to unify tones and keep the whole alive and interesting. This is not a problem that rules can solve. A personal gift for harmony is the final guiding principle. However, rules and systems insure against poor color schemes and serve as inspiration and encouragement.

Color rules or theories provide a basis for solving color problems in original designs. One composition method is "likeness," by which we express our idea in tonal dimensions—value, hue, and intensity—and combinations of these. We may choose a light-value composition, or intermediate or low key (*Fig.* 184). A light harmony would consist of a light green next to a slightly darker green, with the third a step darker. "Stepping" also is used in intensities or hues—a brilliant red, for example, with graduated shades of neutral red. Patterns of color likeness may be varied and at the same time produce an even all-over tonality in a fabric.

Usually we distinguish between the two kinds of harmony: analogy and contrast. Combined tones (intensities) of one color, not differing widely from each other, are analogous harmonies, such as blue and blue-

DESIGN

Fig. 184. Light to dark color values, at left, with check composition in light, horizontal stripes in medium, and vertical stripes in dark values.

green, green and yellow-green. Harmonies of analogy produce quiet effects even when some of the colors are brilliant.

In harmony of contrast, however, larger steps in intensity variation are taken. Oppositional colors are combined. There is a contrast system of combinations to guide us: complementary, split complementary, and near complementary tones. Although these ideas are not fixed, they are guides by which natural feeling for color relationship and textile planning is developed.

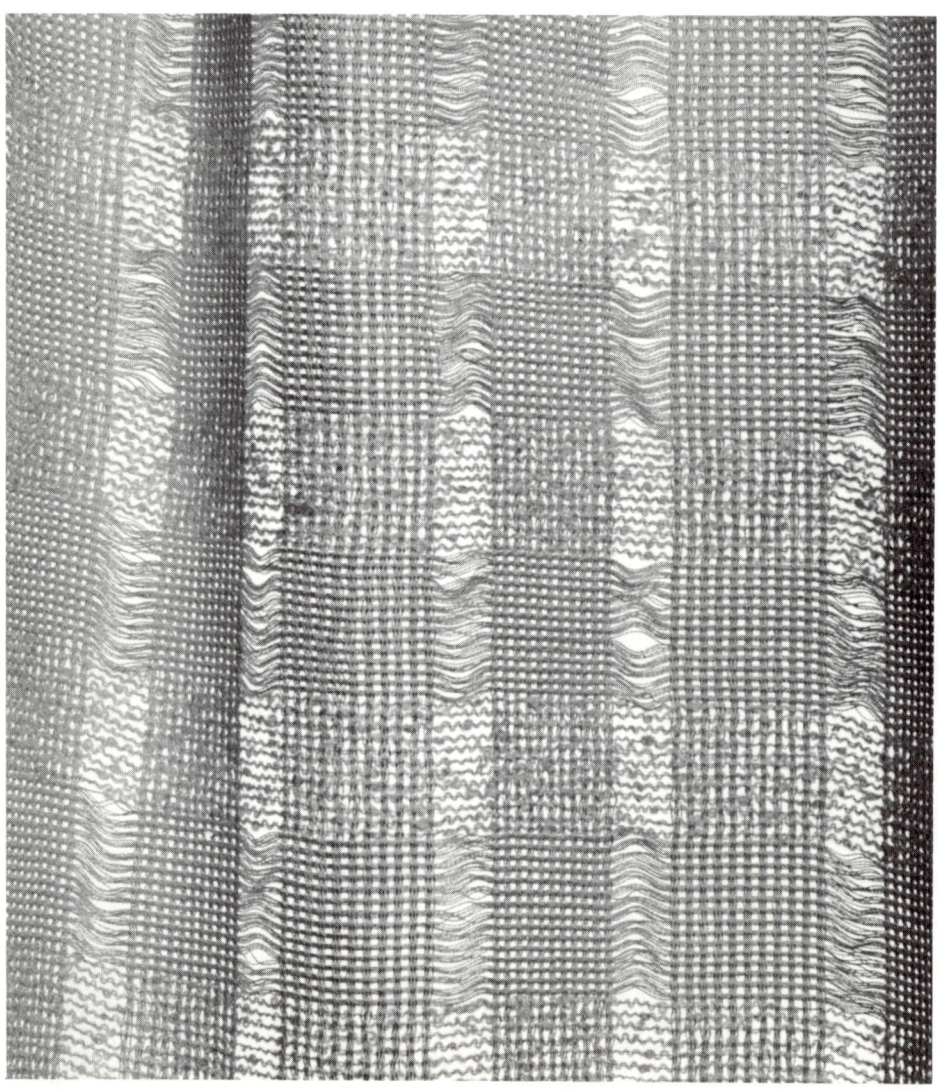

Fig. 185. Textile qualities range from light sheerness to close and heavy stiffness. Lightweight fabrics, like this casement cloth of spun-rayon, require fine yarns and open construction. *Lili Blumenau Design. Photo, Rudy Bleston.*

DESIGN

Weight, or Volume

Most weaving is for utilitarian purposes—warmth and wearing qualities in clothes and upholstery. The designer includes practicality, or weave quality, in his thinking and planning.

A textile may be said to have quality when it is constructed soundly for a serviceable and specific use. The function of drapery fabric, for example, is to hang and fold easily. This is accomplished by choosing yarns, weaves and yarn densities suited to the purpose (*Fig.* 185). A light-weight, sheer curtain will demand fine, lightly twisted yarns in the warp. A pliable yarn—a spun rayon —suggests draping quality, not stiff yarns, such a linen or jute. Sheerness is achieved by widely spacing the warp threads, or, in some areas, using yarns close-up with others far apart. A textile of this kind will be based on a few, fine warp ends and will require a weave that intersects many times. A plain weave—the closest possible interlacing—holds the fine yarns in place. If the warp or weft threads consist of long stitches or floats, the sheer construction loses its shape when hung and tends to sag.

There are no fixed density rules for the different types of fabrics. Of first importance is familiarity with the natures of yarns, and gathering experience of their action when made into cloth. For instance, we may observe that most apparel materials are even-sided twills. We discover that this construction is quite close, but has some floats (non-interlaced yarns) to insure shaping quality. Perhaps the most important construction element the weaver learns is the designation of the number of warp and weft yarns per inch. When you have learned a few good and

Fig. 186. Egyptian covered basket, XVII Dynasty, coarse fiber forming a close fabric, like a stiff-ribbed cloth. *The Metropolitan Museum of Art, New York.*

satisfactory densities, use them for comparison material in further experiment.

Density selection may be illustrated by studying a scheme for a specific textile: a medium-weight textured upholstery, woven in either fine or heavy yarn. If our intention in this is to show warp, a heavy yarn will be needed, as fine threads require more filling and conceal the warp threads. We also must know how thick the threads should be. We learn from weaving experience and textile study the specific and appropriate yarn numbers—a 4/2 or 8/2 cotton in this design would be practical.

When the yarn choice is made, the threads are grouped into a certain number per inch, determining the thickness or weight of the material. An upholstery fabric must be closely interlaced, for it will be stretched over a chair or couch. If too porous, the material will not serve its purpose. Thus 4/2 cotton, which is fairly heavy, may be chosen and used 18 to 20 ends per inch. This density allows flexibility in the material, avoiding stiffness and bulk, which is the result when heavy yarns are grouped closely.

If a fine warp yarn—an 8/2 is chosen—increase the amount of yarn per inch. The finer the warp yarns, the more ends per inch will be needed. A medium upholstery requires widely spaced fine yarns with much filling in order to make a close weave. Uneven warp and weft distribution—18 ends with 30 or 40 picks—will provide insufficient interlacings, and a sleazy quality will result.

Accuracy is essential in choosing the filling yarn and calculating the number of ends per inch. A heavy 4/2 yarn will be chosen if we plan a heavy texture and a prominent show of warp ends. The effect of an equal amount of warp and weft results when we use similar yarn sizes and equal quantities of threads per inch in both directions. Although the distribution of warp and weft per inch may be varied from equal to uneven, equal distribution is usually the rule in heavy fabrics.

In making quality choice—sheer or stiff, heavy or fine—we know the purpose of the material, or are guided by feelings of suitability. We progress from step to step toward the utility of the fabric. Weavers' designs range from sheer to stiff, with innumerable variations, always related to weave and yarns. The sheer materials for curtains and scarves naturally dictate fine warp threads. These, in some cases, are grouped closely, or opaquely, but they also may alternate with open or translucent areas. In many suitable sheer weaves, such as net or marquisette, the warp threads are twisted so that the filling does not slide. This open construction, leno, is highly adaptable to the creation of sheerness and does not require many weft ends per inch.

The tweed materials fall between sheer and stiff in quality and weight range. They are usually made from rather heavy yarns, about 24 ends and picks per inch. In fine worsted, the threads are finer and more picks per inch are used. When we want to weave a stiff material for a wall hanging or belt, the number of warp and weft distribution is uneven. Either a close set warp of fine threads with a heavy filling, or medium warp yarns widely spaced, with proportionately twice as much filling per inch is used.

Motif

The design content of a woven fabric depends on the interpretation of ornament—stripes, plaids, checks. A textile motif is the theme a weaver vitalizes by his particular handling of it in yarn, weave and color. Ornament is part of the structure, not an embellishment, or addition. In the past, stress was on the motif (a flower, for example) and skill to make it naturalistic. Our aim is to

Fig. 187. Principal weave motifs (top to bottom): (*left*) all-over, regular horizontals, irregular, vertical stripes, (*right*) uneven verticals, zigzag, checks, and plaid.

give yarn and weave character to the motif rather than through a kind of photographic realism.

A stripe in various forms and moods—bold or quiet, varied or even—is an ornament. Idea and content depend on the weaver and the purpose of his textile. Some themes are appropriate for decorative fabrics, others for apparel. Fashion and the times govern the weaver's creation.

The simple form is all-over texture, an effect made with any yarn, weave and color. The result depends on individual use or arrangement of the repetition of the all-over ornament. On a warp of one color we may create an infinite number of changes or variations. Take, as example, bright yellow warp in medium size cotton, using contrasting filling—thick or thin, plain or novelty—in close color relation to the warp. To vary the interpretation of the all-over motif, one may introduce a weft thread of much finer yarn and a tone darker than the warp, as well as less intense, such as a tan. A second filling, for further variety, could be in contrast—a ratine spiral thread lighter than the warp.

Experimenting with these two yarns, in the first weave—an even-sided twill—make one row of the light ratine alternate with two rows of the fine dark tan quality, creating all-over effect with variation, a light dotted structure on dark ground. The dotting is the light ratine whose color value makes it stand out. The darker background also has structure on account of the upright warp lines formed by the twill and lending contrast to the horizontal tan fine yarn. The all-over pattern is due to the sameness or nearness of the colors. The interest of the pattern, however, is in the different types of yarns used as well as the order of their repetition at short intervals.

Studying another arrangement of the same yarn on the same warp, we may use four rows of the ratine in plain weave, alternating with the finer, darker weft in a twill of equal proportions—four picks. The design now looks like a stripe, but subdued on account of the close color relation of the yellows. But if we deliberately choose an ornament—a horizontal zigzag—we can transform it in all-over or make a more pronounced pattern. For all-over, we could use two different yarns, or two contrasting colors—perhaps deciding on one plain and one novelty yarn, alternated. This would not show a zigzag, but a textural effect. The same kind of appearance would result if we used two contrasting colors, one black, one white. This would make a bolder all-over impression, on account of the strong light and dark thread.

An all-over design usually is the result of color likeness in warp or weft, or of short repeats of contrasting yarn (*Fig. 188*). Many of these ideas can be woven on one black, one white warp in plain weave, with three kinds of filling: a thick grey, a white rayon novelty, and a black warplike thread.

Fig. 188. Typical all-over weave of varied yarn and color construction. *Lili Blumenau Design. Craft Horizons photo.*

DESIGN

When the black warp yarn is raised for the first plain weave, insert a black weft, making a solid black line. For the next, use the grey filling to create light warps on dark, and again use the grey for another solid horizontal. But with the white warps raised, we may introduce the rayon novelty, then the gray, and three rows of black. The pattern ends with two fillings of the novelty rayon.

This unit repeated produces an all-over of small geometrical effect. You do not see the weave anymore nor show the yarns in their original quality. The colors and special yarns have been arranged to create a particular structure. When the black warp yarns were raised and a black or dark filling used, a solid dark line was achieved. The warp was disguised on account of black on black.

However, if darker yarns are used in the shed for white threads, the warp comes out in pronounced upright lines. Look for these linear effects and not for weave construction alone. Like the yarns or colors, the construction is only one of the means by which we translate our ideas into a design.

Stripe ornaments may be horizontal as well as vertical, and wide as well as narrow. The motif may be achieved with color, yarn or weave. Take a vertical stripe, light and dark components, each a half inch wide. The quality is 20 ends per inch, so we will use 10 light threads alternated with 10 dark. The filling will be the same color all the way through, either light or dark. The weave should show half warp, half filling, as in a plain or even-sided twill.

Fig. 189. Good Fishing Place, 1922, painted by Paul Klee, a watercolor that illustrates organization of stripes, as well as light and dark color values. *The Museum of Modern Art. Katherine S. Dreier Bequest.*

Lengthwise stripes may be woven through yarn variation as follows: a warp quality of 10 straights alternating with 10 novelties, or thick and fine threads, or lustrous and dull. Studying the appearance of a weave, we aim to see and choose contrasting constructions in it. Weaves do not need to look alike. They are often as possible of contrast as two colors or two yarns. A warp and weft twill combined, will naturally provide strong contrasts for stripes, since the one weave has a lengthwise structure, showing a great deal of warp, while the other, the weft twill, brings out filling and horizontal structure. Technically more simple examples are procurable in plain weaves contrasted with length or cross rib. And, of course, we can employ all the elements—color, yarn, weave—in one stripe.

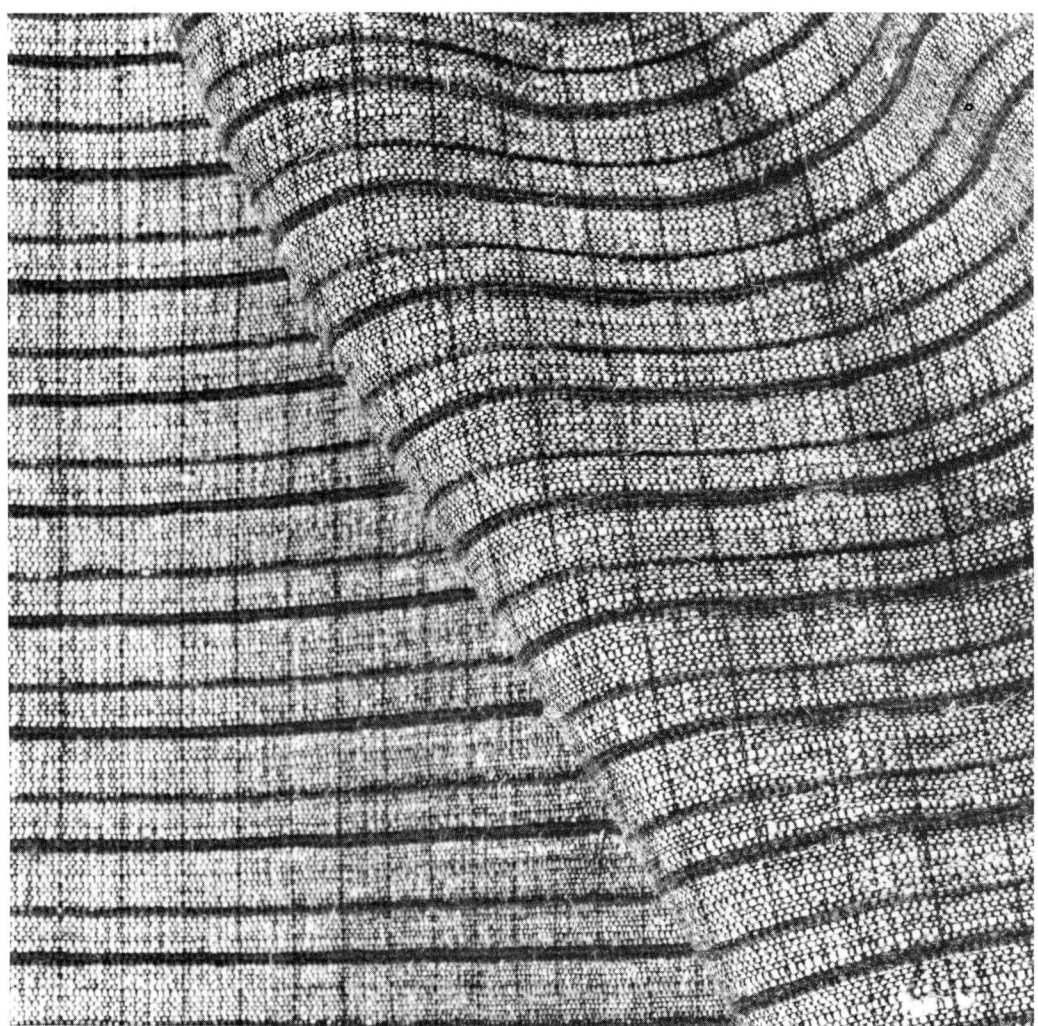

Fig. 190. Horizontal stripes created by use of dark lines on light background. *Jack Lenor Larsen, Inc., Designer.*

DESIGN

Checks and plaids are developed by crossing lengthwise and horizontal stripes, or lines, in a design. The effect is made by contrasting colors, yarns, and weaves. Check and plaid variation is without limit, yet certain factors govern its design.

A basic check is produced by using equal quantities of two colors, or yarns, in warp and filling. For example, make a half-inch warp in blue yarn, alternating with the same quantity in another color, the weft order following the warp proportions—half an inch of blue and the same amount of the other. A basic check is best in plain weave, which brings out the contrasting stripes. Other weaves, like twills, change the appearance of the figure and transform it into a less-pronounced check.

The basic check can be done in any size, only see that the proportions are kept square. A good way to make sure this balance is correct is to measure your filling stripes when the warp is loose, because sometimes on the loom the check looks elongated. Typical two-color checks are made with darks and lights of the greatest color contrast. However, we can make changes or variations within the check. In weaving a yellow and brown combination, for example, we need not use the same brown or yellow in each

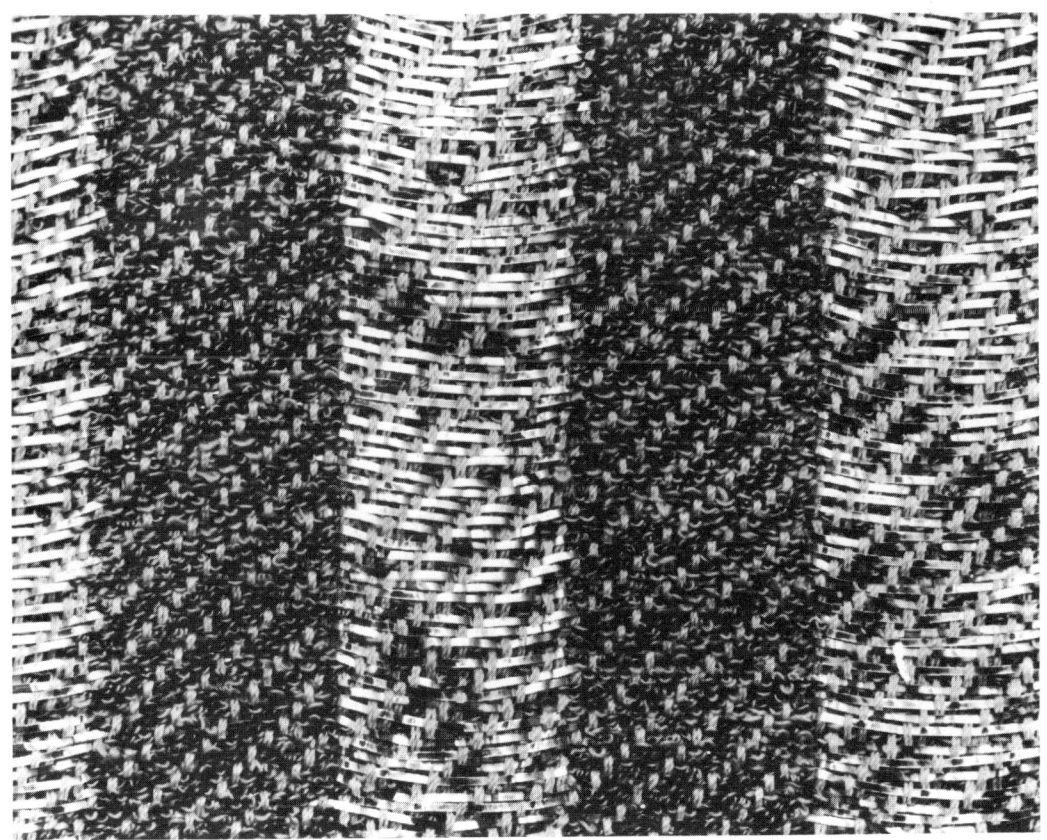

Fig. 191. Equal lengthwise stripes of gray cotton and aluminum thread expressed by means of weave construction. *Anni Albers Design. Photo, Hazel Frieda Larsen.*

stripe all the way through, but design as follows:

One stripe may consist of bright yellow alternating with tan. The contrasting brown division can have two or three values or intensities of this tone. The warp and filling order can be planned an inch wide in the first division, with bright yellow and tan thread alternating. In the contrasting darker band there could be two very dark browns, continued with a lighter, and two reddish browns and another light or medium brown yarn. This order is repeated in the filling. This is only one example of how to go from typical or common patterns toward original ones.

Besides color, checks are designed by means of weave construction. The alternating squares of two contrasting interlacings, however, must weave together evenly. One square made from plain weave and another of 3-end basket interlacing would not work, since the plain construction interlaces more often than the other. However, we can improve this and still make a simple checkerboard on two or four shafts. For instance, make one square in plain and the other in 2-up, 2-down basket weave. This type is

Fig. 192. Checks and plaids, in a Norwegian textile, developed by crossing lengthwise and horizontal stripes, using contrasting colors in both directions. The design suggests many ideas in stripe proportioning. *Cooper Union Museum.*

done on a combination draw. For one row of squares, use straight draw; for the other, the skip draft. For the first check row, use shafts 1 and 3 alternating with 2 and 4. But for the next row, employ shafts 1 and 2 alternately with 3 and 4. The ideal construction for checks of this type is weft with warp twill.

Other check designs come from ways of arranging color yarns in warp and weft. A very old and effective idea is a series of alternating squares in each band—one square of horizontal thread appearance, the next vertical. The equal stripes of warp thread are arranged as follows: light and dark yarns are alternated in warping one band. The last thread, whether dark or light, is used to begin the warping of the next stripe. The design is plain woven and the weft is introduced in the same order as the warp threads. That is, the last weft in one horizontal band must be repeated as the beginning of the following stripe across. A popular version of this pattern is shepherd's check, done with 4 light, 4 dark, in warp-and-weft even-sided twill.

Checks as well as plaids are frequently created by contrasting yarns. Weavers combine heavy cotton with fine, shiny threads—all in one color—in many designs. One stripe can be of heavy yarn, and the other band of fine and lustrous material. In stripes, as in checks, the lengthwise layout in color and material must be the same as in the horizontal scheme. The still more elaborate plaid motifs consist of proper proportioning and the full use of yarn characteristics, weaves and colors for the maximum variety.

Planning

Owing to the technical nature of weaving, a designer must prepare his project before he makes a warp and sets up a loom. He must know what he wants to make—a scarf, upholstery material, or samples and consider its purpose. There is also the possibility that he will be called upon to work on samples for an upholstery or apparel fabric manufacturer. A weaver, however, will often experiment with new yarns to try out new ideas.

As soon as a designer realizes what he wants, the design begins to grow. He visualizes the finished product, considers the technical problems involved to realize it—yarns, weaves, and the set-up of the loom. The planning is both practically and creatively essential. There are no formulas, but there are definite steps which must be taken in the process of translating a design from an idea and graph into a fabric.

Consider a plan for an upholstery fabric. We are obliged to think in terms of an upholstery for use in a room on furniture with which we are familiar. The background in which the fabric will be used both limits and inspires us. Or, we may want to prepare samples for a decorator or manufacturer. In this case we go out, look around, and see materials that are already available, acquainting ourselves with trends and uses of the moment. A weaver who does not live in the large cities will find the trends described and illustrated in home and interior design magazines. No matter how free and independent we feel, our designs must ultimately fit particular surroundings in the contemporary scene. The freedom of our own design and interpretation will depend on how well we know what we want to do.

While considering the upholstery which we plan to design, imagine various appearances that may be given to the material. These idea-suggestions are always analyzed and evaluated in relation to the use of the fabric. If the room for which the upholstery is intended is small, you probably will select an all-over structure, or small, geometrical motifs. You may go over some of your previous work, or samples, finding an idea you have wanted to work out in a quality which now seems right for this fabric. Or you may invent a unit, a small geometric design—stripings of short horizontal lines alternating with verticals of similar length. If you plan a smooth fabric, choose only straight yarns. If you want texture or irregularity, part of the yarns, at least, will be irregular. You must also remember that a geometrical motif is possible only in light and dark yarns. Finally, you begin to plan the color scheme, in subdued, brilliant, or contrasting tones, depending on your concept of the environment for which you create the fabric.

Often you may know, in a general way, the color, kind and quality of the ideal fabric, but find it difficult, or even impossible to get a clear and detailed image of the cloth you want to make. Perhaps you will do best to experiment directly in yarns, with nothing but half-formed notions and feelings to go on. In this way you create samples out of which the desired image will take shape.

In sample making, you may decide on a warp on which you can weave in heavy as well as light weights. You know the ends per inch and have chosen a bright yellow warp suitable for colorful as well as neutral wefts. Having set up the loom with yellow, you begin to see that an irregular basket weave in black on the light yellow warp will look well and be effective. When some of this is woven you pause and judge it. Perhaps, after all, it is too regular or flat. Then, you choose two contrasting black yarns, a straight and a novelty, and try the weave with these. Thus the work proceeds from suggestion to suggestion through a combination of conscious direction and intuition. Gradually you create something you could never have imagined or planned on paper. We discover directly, by experiment in the weaving process, the idea or effect we could not find in our thoughts beforehand. Each way of working or planning has its points. The way depends on ourselves and the purpose of our project. In general and in brief, we decide the best form in which to handle the material at hand.

After you have a certain amount of weaving experience, you will discover the many resources in yourself that come from planning. Thinking and visualization before weaving heighten inventiveness and strengthen capacity to know spontaneously the right yarn and weave for interpreting or carrying out a new idea. Indeed, you will see, in time, that your ideas were already thought in threads and color before you began to weave.

Projects and purposes always suggest forms. The forms, which may be called designs, in turn suggest appropriate materials. We assign to a general idea, eventually, a workable interpretation. When we visualize a certain pattern—a lengthwise stripe, for example—we do not see the actual density of the fabric, but dimensions, envisioning wide or narrow, regular or irregular bands. We may ask ourselves if the construction of the stripes need be of like or different textures. In this way, we really think about weaves and yarns.

By general thinking, which accompanies the planning of every weaver, we return to a specific project or problem refreshed and often ready to solve it. The upholstery for a particular room, which was the example we chose, is first pictured in our mind, let us say, as a quarter-inch stripe of flat and close texture alternating with a raised-effect stripe of equal width. For the first area, perhaps, use linen, and for the rougher stripe a rayon novelty. But to this idea, formed while planning and thinking, you spontaneously add an improvement. You specifically see a very fine natural linen yarn making the flat stripe and a heavy grey novelty in the raised area. And although the color in this design is neutral, actually it has a great deal of color because of the opposed yarn characteristics.

DESIGN

Thus, even before deciding the weave, we can clearly visualize from the warp layout of rough and smooth quarter-inch stripes, the growing character of the material. For our design, perhaps plain weave will best bring out the warp character. The design will be in novelty yarns, and the wefts two alternated shades of grey. When an imagined idea is complete, consider workability.

Sometimes we have to alter a plan after we have searched and cannot find the right materials. However, assuming that the yarns are procurable, we still must figure out the quality or density of the project, and the amount of yarn we will need. If the reed is to be fifteen dents per inch, four dents will have two linen yarns per dent, alternating with four dents, single-threaded, in the novelty yarn. The quality will be twenty-three ends per inch. However, if this does not seem satisfactory, add more ends to the linen stripe, or finer yarn division.

To realize a specific textile idea or design, take time to consider motif, density, color scheme and practical use. As in a meditation on any theme, there is no rule as to which step to consider first. The intended use will often suggest color. Motif and density will be considered simultaneously, because with each change of yarn density, the effect of the motif changes. These are the necessary steps, governed by technical knowledge, weaving experience and taste in planning a fabric.

BUYER'S GUIDE

LOOMS AND ACCESSORIES

Bergman Looms
R. 1, Box 185
Poulsbo, Washington

All sizes of looms, 4 to 16 harness.
Reeds, heddles, benches, shuttles, etc.

Bexell, John P. & Son
24 Patterson Street
Pontiac, Michigan

Swedish type floor looms, all sizes.
Miscellaneous supplies.

Bradshaw Manufacturing Company
P. O. Box 1103
Spartanburg, S. C.

Reeds, heddles, harness frames, etc.
Table looms.

Fawcett, Frederick J., Inc.
129 South Street
Boston 11, Massachusetts

Floor looms, portable, jack type, counter balance (Lar Looms).

Fawcett, Hughes, Inc.
115-117 Franklin Street
New York 13, N. Y.

Table and floor looms, all sizes (Leclerc, Structo and others)
Miscellaneous supplies.

Gilmore, Everett E.
330 S. Commerce Street
Stockton 34, California

Large floor looms, rigid and folding.

Lamalle, Charles F.
1123 Broadway
New York 10, N. Y.

Simple frame looms for adults and children.

Lane Looms
Haydenville, Massachusetts

General agent: Frederick J. Fawcett, Inc.

Leclerc, Nilus, Inc.
L'Islet Station (6)
Quebec, Canada

Looms and miscellaneous supplies.
Agents throughout the United States.

Macomber, L. W.
166 Essex Street
Saugus, Massachusetts

Floor looms, 24 to 56 inches wide, 4 to 16 harnesses.
Miscellaneous supplies.

Newcomb Loom Co.
Davenport 8-3, Iowa

Floor looms, 4 to 16 harnesses.
Miscellaneous supplies.

Penobscot Hand Loom Co.
Camden, Maine

Folding loom (20 inch).
Miscellaneous supplies.

Reed Loom Co.
Box 237
Springfield, Ohio

Floor looms, 2 and 4 harness.
Miscellaneous supplies.

Steel Heddle Manufacturing Co.
2100 W. Allegheny Avenue
Philadelphia, Pa.

Heddles and reeds.

Structo Manufacturing Co.
Freeport, Illinois

Table and floor looms, 8 to 26 inches wide.

YARNS

Acton, Joseph D.
26 Lake Avenue
Swedesboro, New Jersey

Cotton, Linen.

Allied Yarns Corp.
22 West 19th Street
New York 11, N. Y.

Variety of yarns.

Butterworth, Charles Y.
2222 E. Susquehanna Avenue
Philadelphia 25, Pennsylvania

Variety of yarns.

Cliveden Yarns (Dept. 10)
711 Arch Street
Philadelphia 6, Pennsylvania

Wool, Nylon.

Contessa Yarns
3-5 Bailey Avenue
Ridgefield, Connecticut

Variety of yarns.

Cushing Dyes
Dover-Foxcroft, Maine

Dyes for yarns.

Deyrmanjian, D. K.
245 Fifth Avenue
New York 16, N. Y.

Worsted for tapestry and rugs.

Eureka Yarn Co., Inc.
621 Broadway
New York 12, N. Y.

Variety for yarns.

Fawcett, Frederick J., Inc.
129 South Street
Boston 11, Mass.

Linen.

Fawcett, Hughes, Inc.
115-117 Franklin Street
New York 13, N. Y.

Variety of yarns.

Fibre Yarn Co.
840 Sixth Avenue
New York 1, N. Y.

Variety of yarns.

Handweaving Yarn Co.
P. O. Box 7145H
Elkins Park, Pennsylvania

Wool.

J. C. Yarn Co. 109-111 Spring Street New York 12, N. Y.	Odd lots.
Knitwood Shade & Screen Co. 80 Water Street [Dept. D.] New York 5, N. Y.	Bamboo strips, wooden slats.
Lily Mills Company, Dept. HWH Shelby, North Carolina	Variety of yarns.
Welco Brand Dept. H, Division of Wehrling & Co., Inc. P. O. Box 1637 Paterson 16, N. J.	Silk, blends, synthetics.
Yarn Arts Guild Whitestone 57, Long Island New York	Variety of yarns.

BIBLIOGRAPHY

Technique

Atwater, Mary Meigs:
BYWAYS IN HAND-WEAVING. The Macmillan Company, New York, 1954.

Bériau, Oscar Alphonse:
HOME WEAVING. Institute of Industrial Arts, Gardenvale, Quebec, 1948.

Black, Mary E.:
KEY TO WEAVING; a Textbook of Hand-Weaving Techniques and Pattern Drafts for the Beginning Weaver. The Bruce Publishing Co., Milwaukee, Wis., 1949.

Davison, Marguerite Porter:
A HANDWEAVER'S PATTERN BOOK. The Author, Box 299, Swarthmore, Pa., 1951.

Furry, Margaret S. and Viemont, Bess M.:
HOME DYEING WITH NATURAL DYES. U. S. Government Printing Office, Washington, D. C., 1935 (U. S. Department of Agriculture, Miscellaneous Publication No. 230).

Hooper, Luther:
WEAVING FOR BEGINNERS. Sir Isaac Pitman & Sons, Ltd., London, 1948.
WEAVING WITH SMALL APPLIANCES: Book I, The Weaving Board; Book II, Tablet Weaving; Book III, The Table Loom. Sir Isaac Pitman & Sons, Ltd., London, 1922-25.

House, Florence E.:
NOTES ON WEAVING TECHNIQUES. The Arts Cooperative Service, New York, 1949.

Hunt, Antony:
TEXTILE DESIGN. The Studio Publications, Inc., New York, 1951.

International Correspondence Schools, Staff:
ADVANCED TEXTILE DESIGNING. 1948.
FUNDAMENTALS OF TEXTILE DESIGNING. 1949.
WEAVE CONSTRUCTION AND CLOTH ANALYSIS.
WEAVE CONSTRUCTIONS AND COLOR EFFECTS. International Textbook Company, Scranton, Pa.

Matthews, Joseph Merritt:
TEXTILE FIBERS. John Wiley and Sons, Inc., New York, 1954.

Millen, Roger
WEAVE YOUR OWN TWEEDS. Marguerite P. Davison, Box 299, Swarthmore, Pa., 1948.

Oelsner, Gustaf Hermann, and Dale, Samuel S.:
HANDBOOK OF WEAVES (Translated by Samuel S. Dale). Dover Publications, New York, 1951.

Parsons, L. E., and Stearns, John K.:
TEXTILE FIBERS. International Textbook Company, Scranton, Pa., 1951.

Watson, William:
TEXTILE DESIGN AND COLOUR. Longmans Green and Co., New York, 1954.

Worst, Edward Francis:
FOOT POWER LOOM WEAVING. Bruce Publishing Company, Milwaukee, Wis., 1948.

History

Bendure, Zelma, and Pfeiffer, Gladys:
AMERICA'S FABRICS; ORIGIN AND HISTORY, MANUFACTURE, CHARACTERISTICS AND USES. The Macmillan Company, New York, 1951.

Crawford, Morris De Camp:
THE HERITAGE OF COTTON, the Fibre of Two Worlds and Many Ages. Fairchild Publishing Co., New York, 1948.

Flemming, Ernst Richard:
AN ENCYCLOPEDIA OF TEXTILES FROM THE EARLIEST TIMES TO THE BEGINNING OF THE 19TH CENTURY. E. Weyhe, New York, 1927.

d'Harcourt, Raoul:
LES TEXTILES ANCIENS DU PÉROU ET LEURS TECHNIQUES. Les Editions d'Art et d'Histoire, Paris, 1934.
——— and d'Harcourt, Marguerite:
LES TISSUS INDIENS DU VIEUX PÉROU. Editions Albert Morancé, Paris, 1924.

Kendrick, Albert Frank:
: CATALOGUE OF TEXTILES FROM BURYING-GROUNDS IN EGYPT. 3 Vol. H. M. Stationery Office, London, 1920-22 (Victoria and Albert Museum, Publication No. 153T).

Little, Frances:
: EARLY AMERICAN TEXTILES. The Century Co., New York, 1931.

Means, Philip Ainsworth:
: A STUDY OF PERUVIAN TEXTILES. Museum of Fine Arts, Boston, 1932.

O'Neale, Lila Morris:
: TEXTILES OF THE EARLY NAZCA PERIOD (PERUVIAN). Field Museum of Natural History, Chicago, 1937. (Part III of Kroeber, Alfred Louis: Archaeological Explorations in Peru. Field Museum of Natural History. Anthropology, Memoirs, Vol. II, No. 3).

Reath, Nancy Andrews:
: THE WEAVES OF HAND-LOOM FABRICS. The Pennsylvania Museum, Philadelphia, 1927.

Rodier, Paul:
: THE ROMANCE OF FRENCH WEAVING. Tudor Publishing Company, New York, 1936.

Roth, Henry Ling:
: STUDIES IN PRIMITIVE LOOMS. Bankfield Museum, Halifax, England, 1950.

Walton, Perry:
: THE STORY OF TEXTILES. Tudor Publishing Company, New York, 1937.

Weibel, Adèle Coulin:
: TWO THOUSAND YEARS OF TEXTILES; THE FIGURED TEXTILES OF EUROPE AND THE NEAR EAST. Published for the Detroit Institute of Arts. Pantheon Books, New York, 1952.

General

Arnheim, Rudolf:
: ART AND VISUAL PERCEPTION. University of California Press, Berkeley, Calif., 1954.

Carrel, Alexis:
: MAN THE UNKNOWN. Harper & Brothers, New York, 1939.

Dorner, Alexander:
: THE WAY BEYOND ART. Wittenborn, Schults, Inc., New York.

Kepes, Gyorgy:
: LANGUAGE OF VISION. Paul Theobald, Chicago, 1944.

Mairet, Ethel M.:
: HAND-WEAVING TODAY; TRADITIONS AND CHANGES. Faber and Faber Ltd., London, 1949.

Moholy-Nagy, László:
: THE NEW VISION AND ABSTRACT OF AN ARTIST. Wittenborn and Company, New York, 1946.

INDEX

Figures set in italics refer to illustrations.

Acetate rayon, 65-66
Achromatic tone
  definition, 112
All-over effect, *187-188*
  in design, 119-121
Alpaca, 51
Apron, *37*
  definition, 30
  use, 28
Artificial fibers, 62-66
  early, 23-24
Asbestos, 62

Back beam, *33-34*
  definition, 29
  location, 25
Back filling, 101-102, *171-173*
Balanced twill, 79-80, *110*
Basket weave, 83-84, *117-118, 120-124*
Basketry, 4, *4*
Bast fibers
  hemp, 61-62
  jute, 61
  linen, 59-61
  ramie, 61
Beam, *33-34*
  back, 25, 29
  breast, 28, 30
  cloth, 28, 30
  warp, 25, 29
Beaming, 39
  definition, 44
Beater, *32-34, 36*
  definition, 30
  use, 29, 42
Birdseye, 96, *159*
Blending
  wool, 48, *71*
Bobbin winder, 35, *50*
  use, 42
Bobbins, *37*
  preparation, 42
  weft, *54, 65*
Breast beam, *33-34*
  definition, 30
  location, 28
Brocade, *25*
Brocatelle, *24*
Broken draw, 77, *101*
Byzantine textiles, 10, *14*

Camel hair, 52
Carding, *20, 72*
  early, 6, 12
  wool, 49-50
Cartwright, Edmund
  inventor of power loom, 21-22, *28*
Casement cloth, *185*
Cashmere, 51
Checks, *150-151, 157, 181*
  in design, 123-125, *192*
  in weaves, 92-93
Chenille, 70
Chromatic tone, 112
Cloth beam, *33-34, 88*
  definition, 30
  location, 28
  use, 28
Color
  harmony, 114-116
  in design, 112-116
  likeness, 114
  monochromatic, 113
  polychromatic, 113
  psychological factors, 113-114
  value, 112, *183-841, 189*
Color drafting, 93-97
  birdseye, 96, *159*
  hairline, 95, *155-156*
  procedure, 94-95, *153-154*
  shepherd's check, 95-96, *158*
  step pattern, 96-97, *160*
Comb (Reed), earliest, 15
Combination draw, 78, *104*
Combination weaves, *142-151, 181-182*
  checks, 92-93
  description, 90-93
  plaids, 92
  stripes, 90-92, *191*
Combs, *20*
  use, 12
Cones, *55*
Cop dyeing, 70
Coptic textiles, *12-13*
  weavers, 8
Corded weaves, 99-101, *165-170*
Cotton
  classifying, 56
  drawing and doubling, 58-59
  ginning, 55-56, *77*
  grading, 56
  planting and picking, 54-55, *76*
  spinning, 57-58
Cotton gin, 55-56
  invention, 21
Counter-balance loom, 31, *42*
Counter-marche loom, 32
Crompton, Samuel
  inventions, 20
Cuprammonium rayon, 65

Damask, 29
Density
  in design, 103
  selection, 117-118
Dents, *36*
  definition, 30
Derivative weaves, 82-85
  basket weave, 83-84
  rib weave, 84-85
  twill variation, 85-89
Design
  color, 112-116
  density, 117-118
  motif, 118-125, *187-192*
  weave construction, 109-112
  weight, 117-118
  yarn, 104-109
Diamond weave, 98, *140-141*
Distaff, *8*
  origin, 6
Double cloth, 102-103, *174-176*
Draft
  making, 72-76, *91-92, 96*
  what it shows, 73
Draft paper, 73, *91*
  use, 72-76
Drafting
  color, 93-97, *153-160*
  entering draw, 74-75
  procedure, 73-76, *91*
  symbols, 72-76
  threading draw, 74-75
  tie-up, 75-76
  weaves, 72-76
Drafts, threading, *see*
  Entering draws

Draw loom, 15-16
 source, 11
Draws, *see* Entering draws
Dyeing, 70

End, 71
Entering draws
 broken, 77, *101*
 combination, 78, *104*
 point, 76-77, *100*
 selection or group, 77, *102-103*
 skip, 76, *99*
 straight, 41, 74, *93-95*, 98
Evensided (balanced) twill, *110*
 description, 79-80

Fibers
 bast, 59-62
 mineral, 62
 natural, 45-62
 structural, 62
 synthetic, 62-66
Filling, 25, 71
Flake yarn, 68, *87*
Flax
 processing, 59-61, *81*
Float, 99, *165*
Floor loom, *32-34, 40-41*
 counter-balance, 31, *42*
 counter-marche, 32
 jack-type, 31, *43*
Fly shuttle, 18-19
 loom, *26*
Foundation weaves, 78-82
 plain, 78-79
 satin, 80-82
 twill, 79-80
Frame loom, *44*
 use, 32

Ginning, 55-56, *77*
Glass fiber, 66
Graph paper, 73, *91*
 use, 72-76

Hairline pattern, 95, *155-156*
Harmony
 analogy, 114-116
 contrast, 114-116
Harness, 25, *32-34*
Heddle, *33-35*, 62
Heddle, *33-35*, 36-37, *62*
 location, 25
 kinds, 36-37
 threading, 41
 use, 25

Heddle eyes, 29, *62*
 threading, 41
 use, 28
Heddle hook, 36, *52, 62*
 use, 41
Heddle horses, 28, *32-34*
Heddle rod, *10*
 origin, 8
Hemp, 61-62
 manila, 62
Herringbone, 87, 89, *133-134*
Honeycomb, 97, *161*
Hooks, 36
 heddle, *52, 62*
 reed, *52*
 use, *35*
Hue, 112

Intensity in color, 112

Jack type loom, 31, *43*
Jacquard, Charles Marie
 inventor of loom, 22
Jacquard loom, 22, *30*
 invention of, 22
Jute, 61

Kapok, 62
Kay, John
 inventor of fly shuttle, 18-19, *26*
Knop yarn, 69, *87*

Lace, or mock leno, 97-99, *162-164*
Lam, *32-34*, 38
 definition, 29
 location, 28
 use, 28
Layout
 color drafting, 94-95
 making, 72-76
 what it shows, 73
Lease sticks, 36
 use, 36, 40, *51, 61*
Linen, 59-61
Llama, 51
Loom
 blueprint, 33
 Chinese, *21*
 choice of, 32-34
 counter-balance, 31, *42*
 counter-marche, 32
 diagram, *33-34*
 draw, 11, 15-16
 early, 6-8, *22*
 floor, 31-32, *32, 40-41*
 fly shuttle, *26*

foot-treadle, 11
frame, 32, *44*
function, 25, 29
girdle, *10-11*
Greek, *9*
jack-type, 31, *43*
Jacquard, 22, *30*
parts, 25-30, *33-34*
power, 21, *31*
preparation, 44-45
set-up, 44-45
sizes, 30-34
table, 32-33, *45*
testing, 42
types, 30-34
Loop yarn, 70, 87

Making the warp, 38-39
 frame, 34-35
 reel, 38
Mineral fiber
 asbestos, 62
Mock leno, 97-99, *162-164*
Mohair, 51
Motif, *187-192*
 all-over, 119-121
 checks, 123-125
 in design, 118-125
 plaids, 123-125
 stripes, 121-122

Natural fibers, 45-62
Novelty yarn, 68-70, *87*
 chenille, 70
 flake, 68
 knop, 69
 loop, 70
 nub, 68
 ratine, 70
 spiral, 70
Nub yarn, 68, *87*
Nylon, 66

Offset twill, 87-88, *135-137*
Organzine, 54
Orlon, 66

Pattern
 definition, 104
Pawl
 location, 29
 use, 29
Pick
 definition, 71
Plaids, *148-149, 178*
 in design, 123-125, *192*
 in weaves, 92

Plain weave, *15, 90, 92, 95-96, 105, 115*
  definition, 71
  drafting, 73-74, 78-79, *106*
  unit, 71-72
Plaiting, 4
Planning projects, 125-127
Plastic thread, 66
Plexon, 66
Plies, 67, *86*
Point draw, 76-77, *100*
Power loom, *31, 66*
  invention, 21
Projects
  planning, 125-127

Quill, 37, *54,* 65
  preparation, 42

Rabbit hair, 52
Raddle, 39-40, *59-60*
  use, 39-40
Ramie, 61
Ratchet wheel, *33-34*
  definition, 30
  location, 29
  use, 29
Ratine, 70, *87*
Rayon, 63-66, *82-85*
  history, 24
  spinneret, 65, *85*
Reed, *33-34, 36*
  choice, 37
  definition, 30
  early, 15, 19
  hook, *52*
  use, 28
Reed entering, 41, *64*
Rhythm, *178*
  definition, 103, 105
Rib weave, 84-85, *125-128, 186*
Roving
  cotton, 58, *80*
  wool, 50-51, *73*

Saran, 66
Satin weave, 80-82, *111-114*
Section draw, 77, *102-103*
Selvage, 71
  weaving, 43
Sericulture, 52-53, *74*
Shaft and treadle tie-up, 28-29, *38,* 42
Shafts, 25, *32-34,* 89
Shed, 29, *39, 66,* 71, *89*
Shepherd's check, *95-96, 158*
Shuttle preparation, 44, *54,* 65
Shuttle throwing, 43, *39*

Shuttles, 37, *65-66*
  boat, *53*
  choice, 37
  flat, *53*
Silk
  organzine, 54
  qualities, 54
  reeling, 53-54, *75*
  sericulture, 52-53, *74*
  spun, 54
  throwing, 54
  uses, 54
  wild, 54
Silk-reeling, 53-54, *75*
  source, 11
Single yarn, 67, *86*
Sisal, 62
Skein dyeing, 70
Skein winder, 35, *49*
  use, 35
Skeins, 55
Skip draw, 76, *99*
Sleying, *36,* 41, *63*
  definition, 44
Sliver
  cotton, 58, *79*
  wool, 50-51
Spindle, *6, 8*
  description, 6
Spinneret, 65, *85*
Spinning, *6-8, 18-19, 73*
  cotton, 57-58
  earliest, 6
  Egyptian, *6-7*
  jenny, 19-20, *27*
  rayon spinneret, 65, *85*
  wheel, 12-13
  wool, 50-51
Spinning mule invention, 20
Spinning wheel, *18-19*
  kinds, 13
  source, 11
Spiral yarn, 70, *87*
Spool rack, 35, *48*
  use, 35
Spools, 37, *55*
Spun silk, 54
Step pattern, 96-97, *160*
Stock dyeing, 70
Straight draw, 41, 74, *93-95, 98*
Stripes
  crosswise, 90
  horizontal, 90, *142-144*
  in design, 121-122, *189-191*
  lengthwise, 90-92, *145-146*
  vertical, *see* lengthwise
Structural fibers, 62
Synthetic fibers, 62-66, *82-85*
  early, 23-24

Tabby, *see* Plain weave
Table loom, *45*
  use, 32-33
Tapestry, 8, 11, *13, 17*
Tension, 29
Testing loom
  method, 42
Texture, 103-104, *177, 180*
Threading, 41, *62*
  definition, 44
  heddles, *35*
  reed, *see* sleying
Threading drafts *see* Entering draws
Threading draw *see* Entering draws
Threading heddles, *62*
Tie-up, *38,* 42, *96*
  definition, 44
  testing, 42
Transposed twill, 86
Treadle, *32-34, 38*
  definition, 29
  location, 28
  use, 28
Twill variation, 85-89
  cross rib, 86
  diamond, 89
  herringbone, 87, 89
  offset, 87-88
  transposed, 86
  zigzag, 85-89
Twill weave, 79-80, *107-108*
  balanced (evensided), 79-80, *110*
  evensided, 79-80, *110*
  uneven, 79, *108*
  variation, 85-89, *129,* 131-132, 140-141
  warp, 79, *109*
  weft, *16,* 79, *109*
Twining, *3,* 4, *5*
Twists, 67

Unit
  definition, 72
  plain weave, 71-72

Value in color, 112
Value scale, *184*
Vicuna, 51
Viscose, 63-64

Warp
  beaming, 39-41
  chaining, 39, *58*
  definition, 25, 71
  distributing, 44
  end, 71

Warp (cont'd)
  layout, 38, 44
  lifting device, 8, 29
  making, 38-39, *46-47*
  preparation, 38
  putting on loom, 39-41
  threads, *88*
  tying, *37,* 42, 44
  winding equipment, 44, *46-47*
  yarn preparation, 44
Warp beam, *33-34, 88*
  definition, 29
  location, 25
  use, 25
Warp preparation, 79, *109*
Warp twill, 79, *109*
Warping, 39-41
Warping cross, 38-39, *56-57*
  tying, 39
Warping frame, 34, *46*
  use, 34-35
Warping reel, 35, *47*
  use, 38
Weave, *see also* Weaves
  definition, 71
Weave construction in design, 109-112
Weaves
  back filling, 101-102, *171-173*
  corded, 99-101, *165-170*
  derivative, 82-85
  double cloth, 102-103, *174-176*

foundation, 78-82
honeycomb, 97, *161*
lace, or mock leno, 97-99, *162-164*
mock leno, 97-99, *162-164*
twill variation, 85-89
Weaving, 88
  definition, 44, 71
  early, 4, 8, 14-15
  Egyptian, *6*
  evolution, 3-24
  procedure, 38-45
  technique, 42-44
Weaving area, *39*
  definition, 29
  location, 29
Weft, *88*
  definition, 25, 71
Weft bobbins, 37, *54,* 65
  preparation, 42
Weft twill, *16,* 79, *109*
Whitney, Eli
  inventor of gin, 20-21, 56
Whorl, *6*
Wild silk, 54
Winding warp, 38-39
  equipment, 44, *46-47*
Wool
  blending, 48, *71*
  carding, *20,* 49-50, *72*
  classifying & grading, 46

cleaning, 46, *70*
dyeing, 46-48
shearing, 46, *69*
sheep, 46, *68*
spinning, *18,* 50-51
Worsted spinning, 50-51

Yarn
  alpaca, 51
  camel hair, 52
  cashmere, 51
  cotton, 55-59
  count tables, 67-68
  hemp, 61-62
  in design, 104-109
  jute, 61
  linen, 59-61
  llama, 51
  mohair, 51
  novelty, 68-70, *87*
  numbering, 67
  plain, 67-68, *86*
  rabbit hair, 52
  ramie, 61
  silk, 52-54
  synthetic, 62-66
  vicuna, 51
  woolen & worsted, 50-51

Zigzag twill, 85-86, *138-139*
  herringbone, 87, 89, *133-134*